READINGS IN THE CANON OF SCRIPTURE

David Jasper Series

The Study of Literature and Religion: An Introduction

The New Testament and the Literary Imagination

Readings in the Canon of Scripture: Written for Our Learning

The Sacred and Secular Canon in Romanticism: Preserving the Sacred Truths

Rhetoric, Power, and Community: An Exercise in Reserve

Postmodernism, Literature, and the Future of Theology
Edited by David Jasper

European Literature and Theology in the Twentieth Century: Ends of Time
Edited by David Jasper and Colin Crowder

Readings in the Canon of Scripture

Written for our Learning

David Jasper
Director, Centre for the Study of Literature and Theology
University of Glasgow

WIPF & STOCK · Eugene, Oregon

Wipf and Stock Publishers
199 W 8th Ave, Suite 3
Eugene, OR 97401

Readings in the Canon of Scripture
Written for our Learning
By Jasper, David

ISBN 13: 978-1-60608-835-7
Publication date 6/22/2009
Previously published by Palgrave Macmillan, 1995

In memory of my father
R. C. D. Jasper

Blessed Lord, who hast caused all Holy Scriptures to be written for our learning: Grant that we may in such wise hear them, read, mark, learn and inwardly digest them, that by patience, and comfort of thy Holy Word, we may embrace, and ever hold fast the blessed hope of everlasting life, which thou hast given us in our Saviour Jesus Christ.

Collect for the Second Sunday in Advent,
Book of Common Prayer

which is that inestimable treasure, which excelleth all the riches of the earth.

King James Bible

It is an incendiary device: who knows what we'd make of it, if we ever got our hands on it? We can be read to from it, by him, but we cannot read.

Margaret Atwood, *The Handmaid's Tale*

Contents

List of Plates

Acknowledgements

This book is part of an on-going project which includes my two previous books, *The Study of Literature and Religion: An Introduction* and *Rhetoric, Power and Community*. I am not quite sure when or how the project began, and I am even less sure when or how it will end. Its themes, or perhaps obsessions, are the Bible and how it is read, an ever-expanding sense of the complex interaction between the Bible and the art and literature of the West, and the notion of "postmodernity" as a sense of the bewilderment of our times. The subject of violence was everywhere present in my last book, and continues here, since I believe it is imperative, as we sit in our comfortable offices or padded pews, that we recognize the implications of what we are doing as we read and interpret (or pontificate), or of what is being done to *us* as inheritors of a tradition of reading and interpretation.

Some reviewers of *Rhetoric, Power and Community* expressed uncertainty about the position I was purporting to adopt *vis-à-vis* religious communities, or indeed religious belief itself. I had, and have, no answer to give. I write here, I should make it plain from the outset, against the specific background of my experience of the Christian Church, not through any sense of denial of a larger religious vision, but as part of a personal, and therefore inevitably partial, journey. Sometimes one must travel a long way, unburdening oneself of clutter and learning to recognize new signs and directions before one dares articulate anything at all, and maybe one is obliged to admit that the lights are dimmer than one had hoped. Still, I hope, at least, to try and take certain voices and certain insights seriously, lest in failing to do so one renders oneself deaf and blind to the genuine suffering of those excluded, or felt to be excluded, from the celebration which, in the end, lies at the heart of what I am trying to say. Further than that I cannot go.

Many friends will perceive themselves in these chapters, and recall conversations which have found their way into the book: Robert Detweiler, Mark Ledbetter, Stephen Prickett, Irena Makarushka, David Klemm, Werner Jeanrond. Others are too numerous to mention, but my thanks are heartfelt all the same.

I am grateful to the following in whose pages earlier or different versions of parts of this book appeared: Günther Blaicher, Editor, *Anglistentag 1993 Eichstätt* (Niemeyer, Tübingen, 1994), for extracts from Chapter 2; *Scandinavian Journal of the Old Testament*, 7: 1 (1993) pp. 7–16, for extracts from Chapter 3; Ortwin de Graef, Editor, *Essays in Honour of Herman Servotte* (Leuven University Press, Leuven, 1994), for extracts from Chapter 4; *Modern Believing*, xxxv, n.s. (1994) pp. 29–37, for extracts from Chapter 6; *Graphé*, 3 (1994) pp. 173–82, for extracts from Chapter 8. "The Gift of the Magi" is reprinted from *Liquid Paper*, by Peter Meinke, by permission of the University of Pittsburgh Press, © 1991 by Peter Meinke.

Biblical references are taken from the *New English Bible*, unless otherwise stated.

Preface

I am an Englishman who lives and works in Scotland. From where I am writing I can see the beginnings of the Highlands north of the Clyde Valley, just now becoming purple with the late summer heather. On a map of the world you might be forgiven for thinking that England and Scotland are more or less the same, part of a small island divided by an arbitrary line beyond which the ancient Romans were understandably unwilling to travel. In fact the cultural differences are, and for centuries have been, enormous. Sometimes I feel very much a wanderer in a strange land.

Shakespeare is supposed to have written *Macbeth* in honour of James, a Scottish king then ascending the English throne. One hopes he appreciated the grim picture of Scotland given in the play. By contrast, its English interlude, when the orphaned sons of Duncan seek refuge in the English court, is a moment of almost supernatural grace and calm. The Scotsmen find themselves amongst "a crew of wretched souls that stay his cure", waiting for the King – Edward the Confessor – whose touch may cure them.

> A most miraculous work in this good king,
> Which often, since my here-remain in England
> I have seen him do. How he solicits heaven
> Himself best knows; but strangely-visited people,
> All swoln and ulcerus, pitiful to the eye,
> The mere despair of surgery, he cures,
> Hanging a golden stamp about their necks
> Put on with holy prayers. And 'tis spoken,
> To the succeeding royalty he leaves
> The healing benison. With this strange virtue
> He hath a heavenly gift of prophecy,
> And sundry blessings hang about his throne
> That speak him full of grace.

Later imagination sees this as a time in England of unity – the Church and State coterminous in a single fellowship. It is, of course, a dream, looking back upon a world which was, in reality, anarchic, as a time of peace and wholeness.

Culturally, as well as theologically, there is always a tendency for us to look both backwards and forwards to Paradise: a time lost, and a time to be restored. Thus we read the Bible as a story of fall from perfection and a movement towards its restoration, a romance beginning and ending in a garden. Thus the New Testament itself encourages us to read the Old Testament as a history of salvation, with notions of perfection and fulfilment as hermeneutical tools.[1] In our reading of the Bible there is a continual dialogue between openness and closure, between the demands of doctrine and the fretting untidiness of the texts themselves, and this tension is present in the very writings of scripture. Far more important than the Garden of Eden is the continual, repeated sense of disruption and perversity which upsets the longing for the constructed story of a lost age of peace to which, in faith, we may wish to return. Used by communities of faith as theological guarantees of their "story", the books of the Bible are themselves examples of the tension which exists between them as, on the one hand, patterned for salvation and, on the other, cognisant of the confusion of human experience.

The theologian's task is never done. The story of salvation is continually upset by those very texts which give rise to it, and the problem of how we read the Bible is painfully present in the Bible itself. Gabriel Josipovici in *The Book of God* (1988) singles out the Apostle Paul as the primary agent in the foreclosure of meaning on the Old Testament in the planning of a history from the old to the new Adam (Romans 5: 12–21) so that the dream of a new solidarity and participation in the fruits of redemption may be maintained. And throughout the canon of the New Testament, typological readings back into the Old Testament sew together the fabric of Christian doctrine with its fundamental postulate that the Church is the true and ultimate people of God who are heirs of grace and bound for the New Jerusalem.[2] But, of course, this is a process of reading *back* into a previous literature, imposing patterns upon it which struggle with the loose ends of its textuality.

The notion of "canon" implies a sense of unity, solidarity and participation, that sense which our imaginations yearn for in their dreams of unity and wholeness. Scripture itself longs to be canonically sound, yet by its nature expresses the puzzlement of generation after generation that times are out of joint: written to offer patterns of interpretation upon human experience, it continually refuses pattern. As art, it both dreams and is indefatigably, messily, honest.

What this poses for us is a hermeneutical problem of *reading*. I have often rather provocatively suggested to students that the problem with so many "professional" biblical critics is that they are bad readers. In a sense, the biblical texts almost invite bad reading – or at least prejudiced reading. Saturated with the chaos and violence of human history, the books of the Bible nevertheless prompt configurations of perfection as they institute the tradition of theological reading. Why am I so hard on biblical critics? They are too often, I think, in a long line of readers within the Judaeo-Christian tradition who are, in the final analysis, more interested in what lies behind a text, or its "theology", or its typological significance, than in the text itself. In the Bible itself, as Josipovici has observed, "what is at issue . . . is precisely the nature of patterning, of God's design for the world".[3]

For the past two hundred years or so, reading of the Bible has been driven by a particular notion of history, which is one way of attempting to establish a certain objectivity for the claims which are being made. The growing unease with "historical criticism" is born, I suggest, of a renewed sense of the tricky textuality of the Bible. Frank Kermode's important book *The Genesis of Secrecy* (1979) is an excellent example of a literary critic reminding us that narratives are mysterious, not directed towards plainness and clarity, but elusive and secretive. Reading may not just be a matter of "understanding", but the often traumatic, disturbing experience of "remembering".

Actually the fate of Old Testament characters in books such as the Epistle to the Hebrews is one of a profound *dehistoricizing*, a dragging of them out of the confused, confusing particularities of temporal existence, and a setting of them up on to pillars as moral, or theological exemplars in the "history" of God's purposes. My concerns in this study will be to examine ways in which art and literature time and again return the biblical narratives to their place in the mess of experience, exposing the comedy and, more often, the tragedy of individuals who have had the misfortune to become players in the history of salvation: King David and Bathsheba; Mary Magdalene; even Jesus himself. Perhaps, above all, Jesus.

"Violence" will be a word which appears repeatedly in my text. It is a word which is often used in contemporary criticism and so-called postmodern writings. We have grown accustomed to the idea that we live in a peculiarly violent time and century. Yet, on the other hand, for most of us – certainly myself – life is relatively cushioned and secure. What right have we to claim that we are victims of violence? I imagine that many if not most readers of a book like this will be comfortably installed in their studies with, at worst, the next faculty meeting to brave in the morning.

We need, I think, to be careful. Human beings have always been violent creatures. The Jews of the Old Testament, the traditions of the Christian Church, are as guilty of as terrible atrocities as anything we can conceive. What is exceptional about our own time is the availability and immediacy of information: bloody bodies in the latest revolution, starving refugees – are presented to us on television; acts of extraordinary violence invade our imaginings through film and video; books are more widely available than ever before; even the powerful images of so-called "high" art are now popularly present – witness the phenomenal success of the recent Rembrandt exhibition in London, or the popularizing of the murderous plots of high opera. "Art" is becoming again less élitist, perhaps more invasive.

In our comfortable, cushioned lives, therefore, we are also acutely aware of the violent world in which we live. As someone recently remarked, "We are all now on the deck of the aircraft-carrier." In this book I shall discuss how film, art, popular fiction "read" the Bible for us, prizing open the closed world of "orthodox" critical reading of scripture within the academy and the Church. Art, of course, has always been concerned, in the Christian West, with biblical images, but usually under the sanction of the Church. The great Christian art of the Middle Ages adorned church buildings and accompanied the liturgy, performing the function of visual sermons or spiritual guides. But, as we shall see, English drama was born when the enactment of biblical stories in the Miracle Cycles shifted from the sanctuary to the market place and slipped the noose of ecclesiastical control. The recent film *Jesus of Montreal*, which I shall be discussing in some detail, explores precisely the consequences of a "religious" drama escaping from the narrow controls of the Church's authority.

What all this means is that we are being forced to recognize the need to *read* the Bible in many and different ways. Within the theological preoccupations of scripture itself and within the traditions of canonical reading and biblical criticism, there is a tendency and a drive towards the foreclosure of meaning in the patterning of doctrine and the maintenance of the story of salvation. Students of the Bible are taught proper "methods" in the technical procedures of form criticism, redaction criticism, and so on. But we need now to recognize the plurality of reading, the many ways of reading the Bible,[4] by no means all of which recognize the government of the religious traditions guarding the authority of the canon.

The Bible, as certain people in the nineteenth century were beginning to recognize, needs to be read like other books, released from the strait-jacket of its sacrality. The consequences of this perception involve the complication of the reading process: for us the Bible is drawn into the maelstrom of contemporary critical concerns – the shift of attention from author, to text, to reader;[5] the growth of political consciousness in feminism or "liberation" criticism; the crisis of faith in literature and ourselves which we call, vaguely, postmodernism. Its canonical authority, if not vanished (few would dispute the unique position of the Bible in Western literature and art even apart from its theological weight) is now rocked and altered. And one of the consequences of this is the exposure of the raw nerves of violence in the canonical writings from which lectionaries, liturgy and the Church's scholarship work hard to protect us.

Notice how, for example, the recent Liturgical Psalter which is bound up with the Church of England's *Alternative Service Book* of 1980, and used widely throughout the world, brackets out the last three verses of Psalm 137.

> [Remember O Lord against the Edomites
> the day of Jerusalem:
> how they said "Down with it down with it
> raze it to its foundations."
>
> O daughter of Babylon you that lay waste:
> happy shall he be who serves you as you have
> served us;
>
> happy shall he be who takes your little ones:
> and dashes them against the stones.]

Theologically, at least, pretty inconvenient, we might say!

Elizabeth Cady Stanton, in *The Women's Bible* (1895) was in no doubt that the Bible in the Church exercised a violent control over women, and that the recognition of violence in its pages still remained of relevance to a society which, perhaps, had given up the *actual* sacrifice of daughters for political reasons (though perhaps not). As Cady Stanton writes of Jephtha's tragic daughter (Judges 11: 29–40), "we might attribute this helpless condition of woman to the benighted state of those times if we did not see the trail of the serpent though our civil laws and church discipline".[6]

Nor, as we shall see, is the New Testament free from such acts of violation. As in *Macbeth,* we dream of a unity which was, and is, in fact, an anarchy.

In the teaching of literature and theology we have a responsibility, I suggest, to introduce students into the complexity and pluralism of the reading process. That may, indeed, be our primary responsibility. Martin Luther feared "lest we should be burdened with a closed book and so remain unfed".

As I shall try to make clear, I do not regard the notion of "canon" as either simple or straightforward. Nevertheless, a canon of literature wielding the authority of the Bible does exercise principles of closure, exclusion and suppression when read "canonically". We need to be bold in the recognition of different ways of reading, in the exercise of different hermeneutical principles. Contemporary literary theory readily demonstrates the value of different critical approaches to a text, slipping under certain presuppositions and fallacies, becoming more wary, even if less certain.

Any act of reading, of course, involves certain "theoretical" presuppositions, consciously or unconsciously. What I am seeking is a much heightened awareness of the burden of presupposition which we bring, consciously or unconsciously, to texts which are buried so deeply in the fabric of our culture, whether we like it or not.

Why should we not, then, read the Bible through, say, Rembrandt, who focuses upon the *visual* tragedy of figures in the theological stories of scripture? Studying the Bible through the imaginative demands of the visual image leads us to ask different questions, to come with different sympathies. What my own "reading" of Rembrandt over a number of years has led me to ponder is the difficulty of maintaining a responsible sense of the central mystery in Christianity of the incarnation, when our usual "access" to it is so wordy and literary. We speak of the word made flesh (John 1: 14), yet when we see bodies "in the flesh" – in a Rembrandt painting, or even in film – the tendency is rapidly to retreat to the haven of the words of scripture. We follow, in fact, the direction indicated by Helena Michie in the title of her splendid book on women in Victorian fiction, *The Flesh Made Word* (1987). We flee the body in our obsession with a particular kind of literality, in a manner familiar in the Christian tradition at least since Augustine, and before him Paul,[7] which celebrates the incarnation while at the same time condemning the flesh in a language which is yet riddled with *metaphors* of the body.

By "reading" the Bible through the persistent intertexts of art and literature we may, perhaps, begin to face more realistically the suppressed violence which lurks in the chapters of its salvation history, and begin to free its victims to join in a genuine celebration of "religious reading".[8] What I am fumbling for is something beyond what Mieke Bal has called the word–image opposition, an opposition not so very far removed from those desperate, deadly oppositions in Paul's writings between law and grace, work and faith, blindness and sight, and so on. Ultimately these oppositions will dissociate us from ourselves and our bodies in a killing dogmatic textuality which engenders the kind of violence against the body and the individual everywhere present (and too often tolerated or justified) in scripture. We do, undoubtedly, tend to privilege the verbal, and not only in our study of literature, but in our study of the images of art as well. We have not learnt, as yet, to study systematically the interplay of visual and verbal elements,[9] or to assimilate into our human senses the sights, sounds and even smells which contribute to our "reading" and our participation in the story.

From opposition, then, we begin to move towards integration, painfully working through the implications of new, and ever new, ways of reading texts which have become the prisoners of their own canonical authority. Here we can only make a beginning, and show a few signs along the road of a task which will, in future volumes, necessarily become more complex, more interdisciplinary and more theoretically articulate, enlisting the aid of hermeneutic theory, narrative theory, art theory . . . Like Coleridge's secondary imagination, we must be prepared to break things down, to diffuse and dissipate in order to re-create,[10] to break down oppositions between word and image, and, within narratives, to theorize in terms of their organization of events, their art of telling, and their location within a changing culture of language practices.[11]

Many years ago when I began to study theology, I was struck by some words of the late Ian Ramsey, which have kept returning to me in different circumstances and in different ways. They come right at the end of his book *Religious Language* (1957):

> I hope I have made it plain, then, that in theology we talk about a situation which, from the point of view of "what is seen", is empirically odd; a situation known best perhaps in what can be called compactly "worship", a situation which is one of "discernment" and "commitment". If theology is to do justice to such a situation it must exhibit an appropriately odd logical structure.[12]

In many ways, Ian Ramsey's discussion of religious language is both inadequate and outdated, overtaken by the avalanche of critical thinking on the subject since his day. But his main point here remains pertinent with its terms of worship, discernment and commitment. "Discernment" – reading – is an art which continually needs to be learnt and re-learnt in the context of "commitment" – an ethical sense of the importance of such activity. Since Ramsey's book was written there has been at least one major work of systematic theology written from the perspective of worship and celebration, Geoffrey Wainwright's *Doxology* (1980).

Teaching in a religion and literature programme which is committed to developing the activity of *reading* religious texts, and above all the canonical texts of scripture, often deliberately against the grain of "canonical" reading within the tradition, I would argue for the key-note of celebration and worship: that we recover, by the expansion of theology into art and literature, an imaginative and holistic sense of our celebration of life in all its fulness. Celebration and worship properly emanate from a sense of community and wholeness, not from the individual or fragmentariness. They express something of the *reality* of the dream of unity and peace.

So much reading of the Bible, even within the Bible itself, limits and shapes stories in a foreclosure of meaning which excludes too much. What I seek is a difficult and perhaps painful problematizing of the act of "reading" scripture which incorporates the pain and the cruelty, and offers, in spite of that, the possibility of celebration. "Celebration", it has often been pointed out, is a complex and persistent word in the history of Christian liturgy.[13] Harvey Cox, in his book *The Feast of Fools* (1969), identifies three elements which he believes to be universal characteristics of celebration, and which he thinks should always feature in any act of worship. They are: (a) conscious excess; (b) celebrative affirmation; and (c) contrast with everyday life. These are difficult characteristics to sell to serious students and scholars, and perhaps especially those with a proper sense of the ethical responsibility which they bear. They lie, however, close to the heart of this book, which seeks to expand and liberate the possibilities of reading the Bible, to reintroduce us to the availability of its canon outside the communities of faith, and to encompass both the comic and tragic which are so easily lost and forgotten in theology's critical dialogue with the text.

In thus expanding our possibilities of reading, daring to be excessive, we will also expand our sense of worship and celebration beyond the narrow limits permitted in the liturgy of the Church.[14] The reference of "the sacred" will be expanded, since it will be found *in* the language itself and in its capacity for the sympathetic realization of images. Worship will then be less an activity of address *to* someone but rather a celebration of "a mystery that encompasses chaos itself. This may be a faith that even secular humankind can entertain seriously."[15]

And so, as we begin the specific task of this book with a reflection upon the programme of "canonical criticism" in biblical studies, I recognize that its ambition is great: nothing short of offering a possible re-articulation of a theological voice in a world which has too often consigned the reading of the scriptures to the sidelines of a dry, if worthy, academy, or an increasingly marginalized Church. Through the politics of feminism, through film, through contemporary fiction, perhaps one will find a way back to a community of religious readers which is entirely realistic about the pain of our world, yet still nurtures the vision and romance of wholeness, a belief in the "healing benison" of the English court in *Macbeth*.

Perhaps the next book must be a more technical, critical exploration of what is here suggested. For now, perhaps, it is as well that I sit here "across the border" from England, and a wanderer in a strange land. Such a one must find the courage to speak, and tune the ear to listen, and that takes time and practice. We must take care also to listen to the strange accents of the Bible, respecting their integrity, not imposing on them, and speak courageously in response to those accents with the authentic, human voice of our own time.

Notes

1. See further, Gabriel Josipovici, *The Book of God: A Response to the Bible* (New Haven and London, 1988) p. 275; Paul S. Fiddes, *Freedom and Limit: A Dialogue between Literature and Christian Doctrine* (London, 1991) pp. 45ff.
2. See C. H. Dodd, *According to the Scriptures: The Sub-structure of New Testament Theology* (London, 1952) ch. IV: "Fundamentals of Christian Theology".
3. Josipovici, *Book of God*, p. 275.
4. The phrase is drawn from the excellent collection of essays, edited by Michael Wadsworth, *Ways of Reading the Bible* (Brighton, 1981).
5. See further, Francis Watson (ed.), *The Open Text: New Directions for Biblical Studies?* (London, 1993).
6. Elizabeth Cady Stanton, *The Women's Bible* (1898; Seattle, 1974) part II, p. 25.
7. See Josipovici, *Book of God*, pp. 246–7.
8. See Robert Detweiler, *Breaking the Fall: Religious Readings of Contemporary Fiction* (London, 1989) ch. 2: "What is Reading Religiously?"
9. See Mieke Bal, *Reading "Rembrandt": Beyond the Word–Image Opposition* (Cambridge, 1991).
10. See S. T. Coleridge, *Biographia Literaria* (1817) ch. 13.
11. For a useful beginning, see Stephen Cohan and Linda M. Shires, *Telling Stories: A Theoretical Analysis of Narrative Fiction* (New York and London, 1988).
12. Ian Ramsey, *Religious Language* (London, 1957) p. 185.
13. See P. F. Bradshaw, "Celebration", in R. C. D. Jasper (ed.), *The Eucharist Today: Studies on Series 3* (London, 1974) pp. 130–41.
14. See Detweiler, *Breaking the Fall*, pp. 56–8.
15. Ibid., p. 58.

1

Introduction: Violence and the Canon

> *The full force of the change in outlook and argument concerning the narrative biblical texts came in the eighteenth century. First in England and then in Germany the narrative became distinguished from a separable subject matter – whether historical, ideal, or both at once – which was now taken to be its true meaning.*[1]

> *When one speaks of connexity in New Testament narratives one should not neglect the deepest connection of all, the connection with the Jewish Bible. I cannot now enlarge on that theme – the creation of fictive history or historicized fiction by the development of ancient narrative germs. It is a dominant characteristic of New Testament narrative. To rewrite the old in terms of a later state of affairs is an ancient Jewish practice.*[2]

Hans Frei in his monumental study *The Eclipse of Biblical Narrative* charts the development of what we would now call the historical critical study of the Bible in the eighteenth and nineteenth centuries, and the price which was paid for the rise of this technical discipline. Not that it did – and does – not repay us with undoubted benefits and a rich harvest. But what was lost was the sense of the Bible as writing, as text; history replaced story. The pendulum has now, to a certain extent, swung the other way with the fashion of literary approaches to the Bible, introducing a language and terminology from modern literary criticism which still tends to arouse suspicion and even hatred in the hearts and minds of well-bred biblical critics. From a sometimes crude notion of history and an unquestioned faith in the biblical authors and their theological intentions, attention has begun to shift to the text itself, with a nod towards the thinking of Russian Formalism, New Criticism and various brands of structuralism, and finally to the reader or listener.

This renewed recognition of the forgotten, and admittedly difficult, relation between what Jean Starobinski described as that which is written and that which is written about, has brought with it a new concern for the notion of the canon of scripture, and ultimately the development of a whole new "criticism" – "canonical criticism", provided particularly by two biblical scholars, Brevard S. Childs and James A. Sanders. The renewed literary concern and sensitivity of Childs and Sanders is no accident as their interest in the canon of scriptural texts shifts their focus away from a rather primitive notion of historical occurrence to the function of texts within the dynamic and changing circumstances of living communities of receptors, and the hermeneutical tensions which are consequent upon such changing circumstances.

The word "canon" (ὁ κανών) in Greek means, in the first instance, simply a straight rod or bar. In Homer, canons are the two rods which run across the back of a shield through which the arm is slipped. The word was also used to describe a mason's ruler, used in building, or a carpenter's rule. Much later, and metaphorically, a canon (like the Latin *regula*) could be anything that serves to regulate or determine other things. Finally, the Christian Church described first its books, and later its rules or institutes as "κανόνες".

It is clear from even the most cursory survey of the classical evidence that there was never a time of agreement about the definitive authority behind the word "canon".[3] What is discernible in the Greek tradition is a shift in an understanding of the term as one of mensuration (as in a carpenter's rule) to one of evaluation, a shift from the artisan's workshop into moral philosophy. One thing is quite evident. The notion that "canon" simply designates some fixed rule, formula or norm is quite inadequate and far too limited. Yet this notion dominates the energetic current debate in literary studies which is largely hostile to the idea of canon as something exclusive, authoritative, hierarchical and violent towards those "outside" its norms. During the 1980s literary critics as distinguished as Northrop Frye, Frank Kermode and Edward Said each made their contribution to the "canon debate" from either a conservative or radical perspective.

It seems to me that if oversimplification is a danger, nevertheless it is right to criticize the dangerous "canonical" tendency towards authoritative utterance as from a group which is powerful and has clearly made up its mind about such matters as truth and consistency. At the same time, the hierarchical view of literature which is implied in a canon – that some texts are granted a canonical or "classic" status to the exclusion of others – requires a political response which need not simply reduce all texts to value-free likeness. Nevertheless, as Joel Weinsheimer has recently put it in his chapter, "The Question of the Classic":

> The egalitarian shift toward unhierarchized textuality undoubtedly invites us to a salutary broadening of our sympathies to include the literature of women, minorities and emergent nations – as well as graffiti.[4]

One the other hand, there is also a healthy canonical tendency towards, not confirmation of authority, but towards provocation and disturbance. A continuing theme of this book will be the notion that within the canon of scripture is a literary and artistic heart which runs counter to and upsets the institutional demands that the canon be strictly normative and "orthodox". As the Chicago theologian David Tracy has put it in his book *The Analogical Imagination*:

> somehow classics endure as provocations awaiting the risk of reading: to challenge our complacency, to break our conventions, to compel and concentrate our attention, to lure us out of a privacy masked as autonomy into a public realm where what is important and essential is no longer denied.[5]

One of the consequences of the literary turn in biblical studies, of which canonical criticism is a part, is a renewed sense of the disturbing power of those "classic" stories, narratives and tropes contained within the canon (the immense amount of recent attention given to the gospel parables is particularly significant), such that a perception of the power of canonicity within a tradition includes a recognition of the power of the canon continually to subvert the very authority which the canonical literature sustains.

Let me offer one specific example of what I mean. Frank Kermode's book *The Genesis of Secrecy* has itself become something of a classic with the rare distinction of remaining significantly situated in the fields of both literary criticism and biblical studies. Kermode acknowledges his debt to that most underrated of British New Testament scholars, Austin Farrer, participating in the long debate between Farrer and Helen Gardner which extends back as far as the early 1950s.[6] Kermode's thesis is that, while narratives – and he is specifically referring to Mark's Gospel – function to memorialize and explain, they also hold secrets and remain obstinately obscure. That is why they ceaselessly demand the careful business of interpretation, and this endless textual nagging necessitates continual revision of the authoritative status of the canon which contains them. Furthermore, there is a paradoxical tendency – that the more problematic and secretive a narrative is, the more likely it is to acquire classic, and then canonical status. As Kermode notes in a later study:

> The rabbis and the fathers anticipated ambitious modern secular commentary, which really became possible only when certain texts were granted a pseudo-canonical status. And one might almost say that it was a rediscovery of the apparently infinite possibilities of interpretation, and a new understanding of the necessary obsolescence of commentary, partly dependent on the grant of a quasi-sacred status to secular texts, that impelled the secular scholars to look again at the originally sacred ones.[7]

An episode which will feature more than once in the chapters which follow is the story of David, Bathsheba and Uriah (II Samuel 11). Bathsheba is the subject of one of Rembrandt's greatest and most enigmatic paintings. She is also the central character in a recent novel by the Swedish writer Torgny Lindgren, and becomes a bold, feisty antagonist in Joseph Heller's novel *God Knows*. Rembrandt, Lindgren and Heller will be considered in some detail in due course. My point here is to indicate how art and literature have been fascinated by this extraordinary biblical episode, the theological – and therefore, for him, primary – purpose of which is summed up by one major biblical commentator thus:

> its presence not only shows how the ancient texts have no tendency to whitewash, but stresses that God's cause is advanced not through blameless persons, but by God himself, despite the sinfulness of his best people.[8]

But is not this comment itself something of a whitewash? It was Meir Sternberg in his book *The Poetics of Biblical Narrative* who first insisted on the gaps and ambiguities in the reading process of this narrative,[9] and on the constraints they place upon interpretation. I pose the simple question. If our theologian, Hans Wilhelm Hertzberg, has gone in one direction, towards David, with his easy solution, why have artists and writers who have been drawn to the biblical story gone in another – I mean in their fascination with the silent figure of Bathsheba, whose feelings and actions are virtually ignored by the narrator of II Samuel?[10] David, on the other hand, is there granted a whole range of emotions. If the "purpose" of the narrative is to present Bathsheba as a mere passive object of desire, then it is ironic, at least, that a tradition of "reading" outside the commentaries of religious and theological institution turns the story around *her*, her function in the plot exploded in a rich, alternative tradition which is deeply tragic, deeply subversive of theological conclusion and provocative of radical re-reading. The point, of course, is that the narrative, so full of gaps and troubling omissions, both suggests the theology and, in the *process of reading*, upsets its own canonical tendencies to conclusion.

Discussion of the role and nature of the canon of scripture, even from the time of the Pauline letters, has, not surprisingly, been a matter of ongoing concern. Judaism had its collection of sacred books long before the Christian era, which was more or less appropriated by the Church. Clement of Rome, "Barnabas" and Justin Martyr (not to speak of the New Testament literature itself) all refer to scripture, meaning almost always the Bible of the Jews.[11] Integral to the early Church's reflection was a theological understanding of the canon within its historical development, while the Reformation affirmed the authority of scripture. Nathaniel Lardner in the eighteenth century stressed the historical trustworthiness of the canon. And so, within the church, the historical discussion continues.

In modern literary criticism, on the other hand, there has been little or no interest in the *history* of the canons of accepted literature. In 1956, René Wellek and Austin Warren, in their important work *Theory of Literature*, affirmed that "no literary critic can . . . attach himself to so barren and pedagogic an absolutism as that of 'fixed rank' ".[12] A more recent *Dictionary of Literary Terms* (1977) by J. A. Cuddon devotes a mere four lines to the word "canon", describing it simply as "a body of writings established as authentic", and usually applied to the biblical texts.

The more energetic literary debate has normally preferred a stance against the notion of canon, and has concentrated upon the politics of the classroom and questions of academic curricula. The canon, it is generally assumed, exercises some kind of systematic exclusion – on the basis of gender, race, politics or religion. It confirms the orthodox values of some institution to keep cultural authority in the hands of an empowered minority which survives only by institutional control and sponsorship. This may be so, yet canons in literature do persist – we do still read Shakespeare or Milton in preference to their "lesser" contemporaries – and for critics like Northrop Frye canons actually nourish creativity by providing myths and metaphors, images and narratives. Equally, and more interestingly, for Harold Bloom, the canons of great literature generate an anxiety of influence which continues to produce literary fruit. The notion of canon will not go away simply because its authoritative nature is felt to reinforce violent assumptions of cultural, religious or any other kind of exclusion. Canon, indeed, is not merely a repressive notion (though it certainly may be that) but can also be highly creative within a tradition of reception. In Bloom, perhaps not surprisingly, creative acts of interpretation or poetic (dis)continuity, have a strongly midrashic feel to them, in the tradition of rabbinic commentary – a secular continuation of sacred commentary and textuality.

On the occasions when literary critics like Frank Kermode have turned their attention to the question of the canon of the Bible, it strikes me as odd that there is an immediate tendency to slip back into a historical frame of reference which is characteristic of conservative biblical critics. For example, in Kermode's essay on the canon in *The Literary Guide to the Bible,* he gives particular attention to the post-apostolic development of the New Testament, and the establishment of the authoritative stability of the Old Testament.[13] One suspects that he is wary of precisely that element which the "literary" approach of the canonical criticism of Brevard Childs and James Sanders prioritizes, that is, the theological. I suggest, therefore, that the following paradox appears to be the case. "Canonical criticism" of the Old and New Testaments has developed a synchronic approach which is remarkably in tune with major contemporary developments in literary studies, yet argues for the theological necessity of a more literary approach to the Bible. Biblical critics of the older schools in the largely Christian tradition have continued to pursue an historical criticism on the basis of an underlying theological ossification – a refusal to admit that the anxieties of literary suspicion of the canon has any basis, since the Bible contains the "truth" and there is therefore nothing to worry about. Literary critics like Frank Kermode (and, indeed, Northrop Frye) who have looked at the Bible and sponsored new "literary approaches", have slipped back into historicist assumptions because they are, at heart, unwilling to entertain theological questions. My contention is that the intuitions of canonical criticism need now to be more fully worked through: that is, that there *are* theological necessities, but that these may only emerge in readings against the grain of the theological violence of the authoritatively received text, in the perceptions of artists and writers who continue to interact with the biblical texts in the contexts of successive periods.

If ever we are tempted to claim critical innocence or neutrality, or perhaps triumphantly assert critical superiority over those who have gone before us in scriptural interpretation (and I would contend that both of these tendencies are perceptible in the General Introduction to *The Literary Guide to the Bible*), then we should recall that there is no position of non-power from which we can write, read or teach.[14] Reading is always a political business. In a world which is harassed by oppression and exploitation, and where the conclusions of a theology backed up by authoritative texts may be an instrument, deliberate or otherwise, of exploitation and oppression, intellectual neutrality is not an option. Perhaps all I am suggesting is that a new look at the question of the canon should make us more self-conscious, and aware of the necessary fallenness of the situation from which we write and read, and, for that matter, worship, theologize and participate in any community whether of belief or scepticism. Lest we become too immune to the violence which is implicit in any act of writing or representation, we need to become aware of the nature of our modes of discourse – and not least those which are theological – and their ability to displace other cultural materials. The debate between the historical critics of the Bible and their "literary" opponents, crudely described as between the diachronic and the synchronic, is falsely simplified in the interests of defence or attack. Instead, we should learn to read the past as the history of the present – prepared to expose our insights boldly to interdisciplinary perceptions which may disturb any tendency to critical triumphalism or hegemony. An important text for a Church which has invested so much from the earliest days in the image of the body and the family should, I suggest, be Foucault's *History of*

Sexuality (1976), which exposes the modern policing of sexual "normality" within the model of the family, its repression and the elimination of "irregularities" being evidence of the kind of power that coercively operates in our society. An early chapter of this book, therefore, will compare our reading of the "canon" of scripture with our "reading" of the human body and its most intimate relationships in the Western tradition. The defensive theology of the biblical critic will not, I suspect, rest easily on its vast assumptions for long under the piercing scrutiny of a study of the reading process and the function of the image such as Mieke Bal's monumental *Reading "Rembrandt"* (1991). Not that I wish to abandon the theological enterprise. Indeed, quite the opposite. But the exclusivity of the canon of scripture and its perceived theological necessities must be broken and exposed, and a more universal sense of the sacred yet discovered. Assumptions driven by irrelevant accretions of Western morality or modesty need to be driven out, channelling the violence creatively *within* the sacred rather than destructively alongside it, yet warily so. We are well reminded by Leo Steinberg in his book *The Sexuality of Christ in Renaissance Art and in Modern Oblivion* of the proper inclusiveness of our reading and perceiving (and therefore doing). Steinberg writes:

> These, then are my three initial considerations. The first reminds us that the humanation of God entails, along with morality, his assumption of sexuality. Here, since the verity of the Incarnation is celebrated, the sex of the newborn is a demonstrative sign.
>
> In the second consideration, touching Christ's adult ministry, sexuality matters in its abeyance. Jesus as exemplar and teacher prevails over concupiscence to consecrate the Christian ideal of chastity. We have no call to be thinking of private parts.
>
> But we do again on the third turn. Delivered from sin and shame, the freedom of Christ's sexual member bespeaks that aboriginal innocence which in Adam was lost. We may say that Michelangelo's naked Christs – on the cross, dead, or risen – are, like the naked Christ Child, not shameful, but literally and profoundly "shame-less".[15]

Shamelessly, then, we must go on into the moral third reading.[16] Feminist readings of the Old Testament like those of Professor Bal have made us recognize that the canonical text in its narrative condensation and politico-historical thematization must itself be violated to release from its textuality the marginalized and violated victims of authoritative readings and inscriptions. *From the outset* the text may have been construed and used in a particular way, but that should not deny the possibility that the "text" (in its familial relationship with other "texts" of the body, gender and human intimacy) may be larger than any construction of or from it, and that our readings may continue to be stimulated by the continued authority of its shameless, secret textuality.

Later chapters of this book will therefore deal with the *politics* of canonical violence, entering into the debate over postmodernism through the French sociologist Jean Baudrillard's figure of the simulacrum under our present conditions of late capitalism. Neither Christian theology nor the Bible can ignore these conditions which have, as R. H. Tawney long ago reminded us, largely formed its preoccupations and moral defences at least since the sixteenth century and undoubtedly since much earlier than that. No longer, Baudrillard contends, does the code take priority over or even precede the consumer object – which may in this case be a doctrine of religious belief. The code or canon cannot, therefore, be used to defend the legitimacy of this object. But is the alternative the bleak nihilism presented by Baudrillard? For him, the postmodern condition suffers the loss of the traditional basis for referentiality, leaving only a hyperreality, a world of self-referential signs. (Biblical criticism, one should note, has always maintained a firm and largely uncritical doctrine of referentiality.) The traditional society in Baudrillard's vision, dominated by "symbol" and "sign", with their subsequent dominations, can no longer be sustained, and can only be finally released from its misery, according to Baudrillard, by indulgence in unsustainable excess. As he puts it in his essay "Simulacra and Simulations", with an ironic side-glance at Ecclesiastes: "The simulacrum is never that which conceals the truth – it is the truth which conceals that there is none. The simulacrum is true."[17]

I will suggest that the ultimate pessimism of Baudrillard's later writings is not the final word, yet I would not wish to underestimate the importance of his postmodern insights into the power and violence which are resident in normative culture and its accepted writings. In authoritative texts, however that authority be established, come about inscribed repressions of body, mind and spirit that need to be released by a renewed self-consciousness and a broader, more liberal, sense of textuality and textual activity. In so far as art, literature and in particular the novel, are discussed in the pages of this study, I am prepared to use the words of Nancy Armstrong and Leonard Tennenhouse in their Introduction to their book *The Violence of Representation*, that what I have written is "neither theory nor an arrangement of information that adheres to and validates theory but a sequence of readings arranged so as to challenge rationalist representations that suppress the emergence of their own discursive power where fiction reveals it".[18]

It seems to me that to work seriously with the texts of literature or the textuality of pictorial art, or the texts of the modern cinema is to begin to recognize a way through the violence of the canon of the Bible, or the representation of violence which so easily becomes the violence of representation, since to engage in what Harold Bloom would call a "strong reading" (or even *misreading*) and to "violate" the normative, canonical readings, may be to release a text from the limitations of a theological demand or a religious orthodoxy. Mieke Bal's studies of the Book of Judges precisely demonstrate that biblical scholarship, following in the wake of the seductive traditions of the Judaeo-Christian *heilsgeschichte*, reads in a profoundly selective and thematized way, distorting the textuality of the very books which comprise the authoritative canon. Scripture must be violated in order to release from within its pages those victims whom the normativity of the tradition has itself violated. Herein lies the hope which Baudrillard would deny – a hope within the literature and texts themselves, discovered once their textuality has been freed and the processes of reading re-learned even to a recognition of a reading of that which is unreadable. Nor is this without the element of diachrony, since even to read against the grain of a received orthodoxy is perhaps to acknowledge its narrative significance – the dedicated sacredness in the ruin of the sacred truths and the reclamation of theological possibility in a rebirth of images. The irony may be that the proclaimed theological programme of a John Milton in *Paradise Lost* – to justify the ways of God to man in a long poetic meditation upon Genesis 3 – succeeds precisely because as the theology fails, the clue is to be found in the poetic and literary counter-poem of the epic.[19]

And so, giving my attention thus heartily to the creative art of literature, I will discuss at some length the habit of modern writers of fiction, perhaps following Milton in the risk of violation, of rewriting biblical narratives in the form of prose novels. What precisely is the achievement of Thomas Mann in his great rehearsal of the Joseph story, or Joseph Heller in his tragi-comic retelling in the first person of the history of King David? In each case, where "fiction" is not simply the handmaid of piety (of whatever kind), the literary re-telling releases elements in the Old Testament "story" which authoritative readings have suppressed or excluded. What comes across to me in these novels is the note of tragedy so sadly lacking in the triumphant progress of the theology assumed without question by a devoutly scholarly C. F. D. Moule or a Brevard Childs.[20] A Mann or a Heller remind us of the sheer *difficulty* of reading the scriptural texts and of belief in the Gospel and its traditions, or more broadly of belief in any religious tradition. Furthermore, they sharply remind us of the human necessity of reading the scriptural canon in contemporary terms – a collection of texts not fixed by the orthodoxies of conciliar decision centuries ago, but living within the demands of a changing and challenging culture.

My study will conclude with a detailed consideration of the notion of apocalypse, since its potency as a theme in modern literature has been characterized by the American critic Robert Detweiler as "having come into its own via the urgencies of both information/communications technology and the threat of global destruction through nuclear force or ecological contamination".[21] Indeed, although the final book of the New Testament has always tended to hold an ambivalent position in the canon of scripture, the apocalyptic themes of violence and transformation in the teeth of opposition have always held a central place in the Judaeo-Christian tradition, however, uneasily. Thomas Altizer has put the matter simply – as a warning to contemporary Christian theologians and biblical critics:

> At no point has modern Christian theology been more reactionary than in its refusal of an apocalyptic ground, and just as this refusal occurs in every major modern theologian, that is an occurrence which is a reenactment of our theological traditions, traditions which themselves arose out of the dissolution or reversal of an originally apocalyptic Christianity.[22]

Modern works of fiction such as J. G. Ballard's *The Atrocity Exhibition* (1970), or – more politically – the Polish writer Tadeusz Konwicki's *A Minor Apocalypse* (1979), and films will be studied alongside biblical and apocryphal apocalyptic texts in order to release these latter from this contemporary theological refusal. To rescue them, in other words, from violent constraints of canonicity so that their explosive energy may be recovered in a more authentic reading.

We will conclude, therefore, and without apology, on a post-modern note. I recognize fully and acutely that we live in a violent age in which so often those things which claim to work for our salvation rest upon systematic principles of exclusion in our personal, social, cultural, political and religious experience. Such a recognition is, of course, hardly new. In 1972, in *Where the Wasteland Ends*, Theodore Roszak – a hero of my own youth – was still optimistically envisaging "the visionary commonwealth", the vision of the "apocatastasis" which is the "transformation of the demonic forces into the celestial".[23] Few would now place much hope in Roszak's vision. What we need, and most urgently in the prim world of the theologian and the professional biblical critic, is a much tougher sense of the materials which we essentially work with, that is, the texts which have been from the start, or have become by decree, canonically authoritative. And we need to release them from their bondage to allow them to be read in our violent, self-conscious world, so that far from contributing to the violence and oppression, they may offer, perhaps, fragments of redemption (to use Susan Handelman's suggestive phrase) in our self-consciousness, their textuality free to engage dialogically with the enslaved textualities of our bodies, our societies, our creeds. One wants the varnish off so that texts can do what they best, and perhaps alone, can do, which is simply to speak in a voice which is "worth more than many creeds, many churches, many scholarly certainties".[24]

Notes

1. Hans W. Frei, *The Eclipse of Biblical Narrative: A Study in Eighteenth- and Nineteenth-Century Hermeneutics* (New Haven and London, 1974) p. 51.
2. Frank Kermode, *Poetry, Narrative, History*, The Bucknell Lectures in Literary Theory (Oxford, 1990) p. 47.
3. See Jan Gorak, *The Making of the Modern Canon: Genesis and Crisis of a Literary Idea* (London and Atlantic Highlands, 1991) pp. 9ff.
4. Joel Weinsheimer, *Philosophical Hermeneutics and Literary Theory* (New Haven and London, 1991) pp. 126–7.
5. David Tracy, *The Analogical Imagination: Christian Theology and the Culture of Pluralism* (London, 1981) p. 115.
6. For a brief survey of this debate, see David Jasper, *Coleridge as Poet and Religious Thinker* (London, 1985) pp. 145–53.
7. Kermode, *Poetry, Narrative, History*, p. 31.

8. H. W. Hertzberg, *I and II Samuel: A Commentary*, trans. J. S. Bowden (London, 1964) p. 309.
9. See Meir Sternberg, *The Poetics of Biblical Narrative: Ideological Literature and the Drama of Reading* (Bloomington, 1985) pp. 186–229.
10. See, further, Adele Berlin, *Poetics and Interpretation of Biblical Narrative* (Sheffield, 1983) pp. 25–7.
11. See, further, J. N. D. Kelly, *Early Christian Doctrines*, 4th edn (London, 1986) ch. III: "The Holy Scriptures", pp. 52–79.
12. René Wellek and Austin Warren, *Theory of Literature*, 3rd edn (Harmondsworth, 1963) p. 248.
13. Frank Kermode, "The Canon", in Robert Alter and Frank Kermode (eds), *The Literary Guide to the Bible* (London, 1987) pp. 600–10.
14. See, further, Nancy Armstrong and Leonard Tennenhouse (eds), *The Violence of Representation: Literature and the History of Violence* (London and New York, 1989) p. 26.
15. Leo Steinberg, *The Sexuality of Christ in Renaissance Art and in Modern Oblivion* (New York, 1983) p. 23.
16. See below, ch. 2. p. 20 on Paul de Man, J. Hillis Miller and "ethical reading".
17. Jean Baudrillard, "Simulacra and Simulations", in *Selected Writings*, ed. Mark Poster (Cambridge, 1988) p. 166.
18. Armstrong and Tennenhouse, *Violence of Representation*, p. 9.
19. The term "counter-poem" is used by David Daiches in his chapter on *Paradise Lost* in *God and the Poets* (Oxford, 1984) to designate the dramatic "subtlety, ambiguity [and] multiple suggestiveness" which run counter to the overt theology of Milton's argument. This is to argue against the proposals of David Tracy in *The Analogical Imagination* (London, 1981) pp. 200–1, where he suggests that "on purely literary grounds, Milton's Satan is far more successful than Milton's God; and yet, contra Blake and Empson, this is not the final clue to the religious vision of *Paradise Lost*". In this instance, at least, I suggest that Blake and Empson are better readers and more perceptive than their theological successor in Milton studies.
20. For a development of this hint, see below, ch. 2, p. 18, etc.
21. Robert Detweiler, "Apocalyptic Fiction and the End(s) of Realism", in *European Literature and Theology in the Twentieth Century*, eds David Jasper and Colin Crowder (London and New York, 1990) p. 154.
22. Thomas J. J. Altizer, *Genesis and Apocalyptic: A Theological Voyage Toward Authentic Christianity* (Louisville, 1990) pp. 9–10.
23. Theodore Roszak, *Where the Wasteland Ends: Political and Transcendence in Post Industrial Society* (1972; London, 1974) ch. 13, "Apocatastasis", pp. 446–65.
24. See Harold Bloom, *The Book of J* (London, 1991) p. 44. I will discuss this work in some detail later, regarding it as a particularly important and perceptive example of fictional writing. That is not meant as an insult to its scholarship. Quite the contrary.

2

Trespassing in the Wilderness: New Ventures in Canonical Criticism

In *The Oxford Dictionary of the Christian Church,* Marcion (d.c.160) is described in just one word – "heretic". He was, according to Hippolytus, the son of a bishop who excommunicated him on grounds of immorality. Arriving in Rome about 140 CE, he attached himself to the church there until again he was excommunicated in 144. Earning the combined hatred of Irenaeus (who wrote of Marcion's "daring blasphemy"), Justin Martyr, Tertullian and the historian Eusebius, Marcion taught that the Christian gospel was wholly a gospel of love, to the complete exclusion of the Law. He rejected in its entirety the Old Testament since its Jewish God was, according to Marcion, despotic, cruel and ignorant. He was, in short, utterly different from the God of love who is revealed in Jesus. Canonically all that Marcion acknowledged of the Bible was the Pauline epistles (excluding the Pastoral epistles, I and II Timothy and Titus), and an edited form of Luke's Gospel. It comes as something of a shock, therefore, when a distinguished contemporary biblical scholar suggests that: "Christianity has become so systematically Marcionite and anti-Semitic that only a truly radical revival of the concept of canon as applied to the bible will, I think, counter it."[1]

We return, then, to an ancient debate, a revival of a necessary concept which is found, even there problematically, in the New Testament itself. The author of the Second Epistle of Peter places Paul's "inspired" writings on a level with "other scriptures" (τὰς λοιπὰς γραφὰς), that is, the Old Testament, though both "contain some obscure passages, which the ignorant and unstable misinterpret to their own ruin" (II Peter 3: 16). The canon of inspired writings, therefore, is both necessary and dangerous, calling for careful interpretation and hermeneutic practice. By the time of Irenaeus (*c.*130–*c.*200), the fully scriptural character of the specifically Christian writings was universally established and their designation as "New Testament" acknowledged.[2]

James Sanders's call for a revival of the concept of canon in the contemporary practice of so-called "canonical criticism" is a recognition that even in the New Testament itself there are Marcionite and anti-Semitic tendencies, or, more generally, the dangers inherent in any process of establishing and stabilizing a library of authoritative texts. For Sanders is quick to acknowledge that stabilized texts, and sacred texts in particular, are peculiarly susceptible to the misreading alluded to in II Peter unless what he calls "appropriate hermeneutics" are employed to ensure the dynamic analogy relative to *text*, and sociological and historical *context*.[3] The "concept of canon", therefore, must be tensioned between the sense of stability and the sense of adaptability, the tension being maintained by a relentless hermeneutic awareness. It may be necessary for the like of the canon to "do violence"[4] to its text, which is not to take it less than seriously in its entirety, but fully to engage with it, questioning it and being questioned by it as the necessary condition of its canonicity.[5] Only then may one hope to escape from what James G. Williams has described as the "myth of sanctioned violence", a violence quickly and devastatingly apparent in the anti-Semitism which is the characteristic of Marcion's God of love, expressed in the insistent traditions of persecution and pogrom.

Proper attention to the Bible within the Judaeo-Christian tradition, both Old Testament and New Testament, cannot avoid the serious question of canonicity. For all his massive scholarly achievement, I am therefore deeply suspicious of the little space given to this question by Rudolf Bultmann in his *Theology of the New Testament*, where he suggests that the canon is essentially a fourth-century issue linked to the development of the office of the bishop in the Church as an effort to secure right doctrine through the weight of written tradition. Bultmann concludes that "unity of doctrine was assured by the canon".[6] The huge assumptions which underlie this conclusion have evoked an overt and persistent violence in the history of the Christian Church which is matched by the covert, and in some ways more insidious, violence of the long-prevailing historical-critical scholarship of the Bible with its insistent belief in the dogma of a value-neutral, detached interpretation of texts.

Such fastidious and energetically defended scholarly detachment is described by Elizabeth Schüssler Fiorenza as "historically understandable . . . [but] theoretically impossible". Fiorenza's own position is dominated by her *political* sense of the task of biblical interpretation, far removed from the so-called objectivity and freedom from values of academic scholarship – but an energetic pursuit of the text in "its apologetic-political setting and function of legitimization".[7] The politics of feminism since Elizabeth Cady Stanton and *The Woman's Bible* (1895, 1898) has played an increasingly important role in the appreciation of the nature of canonicity, alongside other "liberation theologies" of the oppressed and exploited. But at the risk of seeming over-cautious, it behoves us initially to pause awhile and consider in some detail the critical questions posed for interpretation and biblical scholarship by the two principal exponents of so-called "canonical criticism", Brevard S. Childs and James A. Sanders. On the basis of these questions, duly raised and assessed, we may become better equipped to trespass in a scholarly wilderness where, if the desert is often dry and dusty, one should always recall that there the great battles of biblical theology are usually fought and won, even if the prospect of a forty-year sojourn seems initially daunting!

A general point first. Brevard Childs begins his weighty study *The New Testament as Canon* with a timely reminder. He writes:

> Although the attempt to sketch the broad lines of a new vision of the text can never be a substitute for the detailed, painstaking research of the biblical scholar, such technical work can easily run into the sand if the larger concept of the enterprise has been lost.[8]

The sands of the desert may, indeed, rapidly engulf us if we fail to direct our gaze to the larger vision or risk a slow and painful intellectual – not to say spiritual – death in the dry woods of pedantic minutiae. James Sanders goes further in reminding us that if canonical criticism finds an ally in literary critical holistic readings of the Bible, it goes further still in its narrative analysis of biblical intertextuality and its recognition and affirmation of the monotheizing process which the Bible describes.[9] A timely reminder, and a warning: for if the broad vision is always to be defended against pedantry, Child's specific theological motive and Sanders's frankly unquestioned theological naivity, voiced from within the communities of the faithful, situate theology, and specifically Christian theology, uncomfortably as a *given*, working from and toward God as the sole given,[10] rather than recognizing that, contrary to their own intentions, their concerns necessitate, theologically, a more literary approach to the Bible.[11] That is, canonical criticism, taken to its proper conclusions, suggests a hermeneutic freedom in reading which *may*, ultimately, be the ground of theological discovery and a genuinely new theological insight, but actually damages theology when its imposition upon the text serves to distort the processes of criticism.

Let me offer some examples of what I mean. In his book *Old Testament Theology in a Canonical Context*, Brevard Childs claims that his canonical approach "opens an avenue into the material in order to free the Old Testament for a more powerful theological role within the life of the Christian Church".[12] For Childs, Old Testament theology is essentially a Christian discipline, its interpretation and appropriation sharing certain features deriving from Christian theology. What sort of critical freedom is this, bound within the assumptions of an exclusive tradition which is ultimately alien to the Jewish writings themselves, and working *from* theology, not – more creatively – *towards* theology? Thus, working with this constriction, Childs undercuts his own literary insights when he raises, quite properly, the problem of referentiality in historical criticism of the Bible, and then limits the critical question by enlisting the categorical claims of a "theological reality".[13] James Sanders, who, in many respects, is more interesting than Childs in his more subtle relationship with historical-critical methods, limits his programme by an overtly pastoral purpose. As he puts it, most succinctly:

> The canonical paradigm shows how believing communities may learn to hear the voice of God from outside the inner community traditions. The Bible as canon is a veritable textbook of hermeneutics on how to adopt and adapt wisdom from any part of God's creation.[14]

Is the "voice" of the text, or of the reading process, therefore to be equated simply with the "voice of God"? Is the process of reception merely to be one of adoption and adaptation of a particular "wisdom"? Such assumptions, I would argue, are quickly problematized in the history of the politics of biblical reception, in which stances of interpretation may rapidly legitimate a power of oppression or a sanctioned violence, in God's name.

A final example of what I mean may be found on the last page of C. F. D. Moule's hugely influential study *The Birth of the New*

Testament, a work noted with approval by Brevard Childs. At heart an old-fashioned form critic, Moule nevertheless views the literature of the New Testament as the early Church's attempt to explain itself theologically in various stages of self-awareness. Fine – were it not for his concluding remark: "That it is also the tale of a divine overruling of the gropings and mistakes of men is here assumed without further ado."[15] An example, perhaps, of the will to believe, but what of the critical spirit?

Both Childs and Sanders identify the work of J. S. Semler, *Abhandlung von freier Untersuchung des Canons* (1771–5), as the inauguration of modern study of the biblical canon. Semler's approach to the subject was uncompromisingly historical and distinct from the traditional dogmatic, apologetic concept of canon. He delved behind notions of normativity and anticipated much of the more recent work of historical critical methods with his concentration upon the liturgical context of the earliest Christian writings. Semler's emphasis is almost exclusively on stability rather than adaptability.

Childs and Sanders share a move away from the dominant historicism of biblical criticism, though each in different ways embark upon essentially historical critical tasks. Childs rejects historicist readings of biblical texts which:

> Assume that the meaning of a text derives only from a specific historical referent. [They seem] unaware that the function of canonical shaping was often precisely to loosen the text from any one given historical setting, and to transcend the original addressee. The very fact that the canonical editors tended to hide their own footprints, largely concealing their own historical identity, offers a warrant against this model of historical reconstruction.[16]

Much here might cause the literary critic gratefully to prick up her ears in the shift from the diachronic to the synchronic, the recognition of the hermeneutical problem of the identity of the "reader", or addressee, and the dissolution of the identity of the editor, not to speak of the author. Attention is shifted from the particularities of the apostolic age to the canonical literature as it is used within a community of faith and practice, shifted, in other words, from a predominantly historical paradigm to a predominantly literary one. Childs in particular concentrates on the final form of the text, and, drawing upon a comparison with the literary discoveries at Nag Hammadi and the Dead Sea, suggests that "the struggle to define the nature of the gospel did not follow the fixing of the New Testament, but was an integral part of the process in which the decisions of the early church regarding canonicity were made".[17] His approach, in other words, is synchronic, concentrating on the community which actually produced and used the text, rather than the historical circumstances from which it presumably emerged, or the later often conciliar attitudes towards it and its authority, the issue at stake turning on "establishing a stance from which the Bible is to be read as Sacred Scripture".[18]

James Sanders's canonical project both develops that of Brevard Childs and further emphasizes the theological problem. Sanders's historical frame of reference shifts from the history of Israel, from the time of Christ and from the apostolic age, to the ongoing history of the biblical literature itself. Though he continues to focus on the origins of the canon, Sanders recognizes that "it is the nature of canon to be contemporized"[19] and from this ever-changing context an energetic canonical hermeneutics is given two basic tasks: (a) to determine legitimate ways of establishing the meaning of a biblical text in its own setting, and (b) to establish a proper mode of expression of that meaning in developing contemporary settings.[20] Sanders, while granting particular emphasis to the historical time which gave the canon its basic shape, also recognizes the developing conditions of reception – that canonical hermeneutics must shift attention away from the notion of a text stabilized by the imposition of the structures, intentions and cultural systems of a particular moment in its history, towards the history of its reception within the communities of faith. He is thus somewhat less susceptible than Childs to the dangers of a theological motive which dictates a "canonical shape" – that, for example, as we have seen, Old Testament theology is essentially a Christian discipline which arbitrarily separates the Old from the New Testament – a framework which is ultimately damaging to theology because it tends towards another myth of sanctioned violence.

With their different emphases, Childs and Sanders are at once more and less "historical" than the tradition of historical criticism of the Bible which they set out to criticize. They represent a shift from the particularity of establishing the specific historical reference of the biblical texts in the history of Israel or the life of Christ. But at the same time they recognize the special relationship between scripture and the historical communities which shaped (and continue to shape) its literature, and conversely the effect of the Bible on the self-understanding of those communities. They represent, in other words, a shift from the particular to the universal. To give a specific example, the contention that from a "canonical perspective" the imagery of the Man from heaven in the Fourth Gospel can neither be demythologized, nor historicized, nor "rendered into a mute sociological force",[21] presents the alternative of its function as a Christological paradigm. In Sanders's criticism we find emphasized an understanding of the Bible altogether as canon, "as a paradigm on how to monotheize over against all kinds and sorts of polytheism, or fragmentations of truth".[22] The shift into the broader sense of historical reference encourages the establishment of paradigms in a manner not so very far removed from the structuralist interest in discovering the "deep structure" of a text, which is known through the interplay of metonymy and metaphor, that is, the recognition of paradigmatic patterns embedded in the syntagm of the surface discourse.[23] The difference in Childs and Sanders is their linking of the paradigms to their theological assumptions which are, in turn, historicized in the life of particular groups and communities. Thus, though Sanders, at least, recognizes a hermeneutics as the midterm of the axis between stability and adaptability, even he fails to take the final, radical step of a necessary, destabilizing reading against the grain which, arguably both text and canon invite, and which, in Paul de Man's terms "upsets rooted ideologies by revealing the mechanics of their workings".[24] Going as far as recognizing that the canon consists of the *interpreted*, and continually interpreted, text, does not escape the consequences of failing to admit the ethical necessity of reading the "unreadability" of text. Here it may be helpful to refer to J. Hillis Miller's commentary on de Man's chapter in his book *Allegories of Reading*, entitled "Allegory (*Julie*)". Miller writes:

> The first feature of the ethical for de Man, then, is that it is an aspect not of the first narrative of metaphorical denomination, nor of the second narrative of the deconstruction of that aberrant act of denomination, but of the "third" narrative of the failure to read which de Man calls "allegory".[25]

Canonical critics recognize de Man's first narrative and, to a degree, also the second. What they clearly fail to do is take the ethical step into the third narrative, rooted as they are in the prior claims of theology. Only this ethical step into the unknown can suggest the radically new possibility of a theology rediscovered – a truly post-modern theology, born from the ashes of our necessary failure to "read" the old. Only thus do we begin to perceive that in the canon of scripture there is a deeply rooted violence which is bred by the authoritatively received text, however one understands that term: and the only way to expose this violence is to learn to read these canonical texts against the grain – against the grain of their canonicity and against the grain of their invitation to interpret within the tradition.

Brevard Childs's brief excursus in *The New Testament as Canon*[26] on George A. Lindbeck's book *The Nature of Doctrine* illuminates a number of the points which I have been trying to make. Welcoming though he is to the "cultural-linguistic" approach of Lindbeck's theology, Childs's reservations are precise and predictable. He acknowledges the stress placed by Lindbeck on the need to ground reception in the community of Christian faith and practice, as also the significance of "an intratextual context for a community of faith".[27] Actually Lindbeck's discussion of intratextuality[28] is simply another version of structuralism in the semiotic system of a dogmatic theology. From this Childs draws back at the point when theological – as opposed to historical – referentiality is in danger of being destabilized. He also fears Lindbeck's critical notion of doctrine functioning as an instantiation of rules and is provoked into confessing his deeply conservative religious belief based on the "cognitive or experiential dimensions of the canon".

What is striking to me as a literary critic in the two canonical critics of the Bible with whom we have been concerned is the repeated resonances in their work of recent and current issues in literary criticism and theory. In contrast to the disintegrative tendencies of so much biblical criticism, with its tendency to eliminate and prioritize elements to suit its own game, canonical criticism is committed to dealing with texts as they are received in the canon. As Childs has expressed it in his criticism of the work of Joachim Jeremias on the parables:

> The various elements of growth, embellishment, and alteration which Jeremias has so carefully described should not be dismissed

> as distorting accretion, but rather considered as an aid in understanding the special nature of the church's construal of Jesus' message.[29]

Starting from this sense of the *integrity* of the text, Childs reminds us that there is no one correct point of critical entry, but many forms and levels of the task of biblical exegesis.

The issue of authorial *intentionality* is met when it is quickly realized that the attempt to ground a scriptural text in the intentionality of an author fails to reckon with the problem of canon. The prophetic books, or the gospels, may not simply have been written by different authors, bur perhaps more significantly have been received and transmitted by different readers and audiences over long periods of time.

Referentiality also becomes a critical issue when the essentially crude theory of historical referentiality which has dominated biblical studies since the Enlightenment is replaced in canonical criticism by referentiality of a theological order.

The recognition of the part played by continuing and ongoing communities of readers and listeners is a continuous reminder that the establishment of *meaning* is not dependent on the recovery of a lost key, but is a ceaseless hermeneutical task concerned with the contexts in which biblical texts were and are read as much as with the texts themselves.

On the other hand, the *structuralist* tendencies in canonical criticism which I have already described indicate the shift from an interest in author and intention to a focus on the text itself. Indeed, Childs and Sanders well represent that shift in biblical studies which follows the long-recognized shift in literary studies from author, to text, to reader, each emphasis tending to superimpose itself upon the previous one rather than displace it.[30]

Finally, the development of what James Sanders calls "canonical hermeneutics" indicates a sense in common with almost all critical theory that the task of understanding and properly exercising the business of interpretation which was reinvigorated for us by the work of Friedrich Schleiermacher must again be taken with the utmost seriousness by biblical scholarship recognizing its contemporary hermeneutical responsibilities in the ancient line of tradents who themselves read and re-presented authoritative traditions whether oral or written.

Wherein, in conclusion, therefore, lies the problem with this particular and often critically sophisticated contribution to the much more widespread contemporary canon debate in literary studies? My answer to that question is essentially very simple. Contrary to the explicit theological intentions of Childs and Sanders, they actually bear witness to the theological necessity of a more, and more specifically, literary approach to scripture.[31] That is, they have got things the wrong way round: we need to work not *from* an initial theological framework, but more daringly *towards* a theological possibility through a broadly interpretative recognition of the reception of the biblical canon both within and outside the communities of the faithful, in art, literature and the political acts of those struggling in wildernesses of alienation and marginalization. The alternative is an inevitable critical dissolution in the overt or covert structures of what, for Christians at least, Stephen Moore has challengely designated "God's own (Pri)son".[32] Ray L. Hart describes it thus:

> Just this dissolution is theological pantheism, the homing instinct of the "religious" temperament. Such theology, both in principle and in performance, is a dehumanizing and a detemporalizing enterprise. Its derogation of humanity is achieved precisely by means of preoccupation with *God*. In fact, it *illustrates* "original sin" through its preoccupation with God in the way that only God can be preoccupied with himself.[33]

My broad concern, in the light of my critique of the project of canonical criticism of the Bible, is to expand the study of the reception of the scriptural canon both within and outside the Judaeo-Christian tradition in the West. I have already outlined some of the preoccupations of the subsequent chapters of this book in Chapter 1. Here I want briefly to review that discussion again in the light of our more detailed reflection upon the work of Childs and Sanders. I want to expand the sense of the difficulties of interpreting the Bible in the context of the highly politicized concerns of feminism as one example of the experience of the canon under the challenge of the marginalized or those who feel themselves to be marginalized. In the secularized world of contemporary criticism the note is often sounded that "the canon" operates simply as an instrument of principled, systematic exclusion.[34] What then of its continuance under the blows of the excluded, whether these be women, or racial minorities, or the legions of underprivileged and downtrodden? Or may it be rather a hermeneutic issue – that the life of the scriptural canon needs a violence to liberate it from the dangers of its own myth of sanctioned violence? Brevard Childs himself acknowledges that he uses the term canon in a number of different ways; as a normative, fixed body of literature within the Church, as a particular theological construal of the tradition, and as the interpretative activity of the modern Christian reader.[35] I would wish to expand and develop this multiplicity still further in order to preserve the vibrancy of the texts within a living, widely relevant tradition.

What then of the vast tradition of "reading" the Bible in the images of art, by artists using the Bible for many purposes – to sanction protest, to express piety, to represent tragedy, to explore the human condition, either *sub specie aeternitate* or not? This tradition, it seems to me, is a further and still vibrant element in the history of the canon. Not least, the pictorial image or three-dimensional sculpture forces us to consider the image of the body as a central and too often utterly neglected element in a religious and theological tradition in the Christian Church which, on the one hand celebrates an incarnation, but, on the other, has systematically either excluded "the body" from its moral parameters, or worse, tortured the body for the good of the soul.

From art I would move onwards to the contemporary experience of the Bible in the cinema – a medium which raises acute questions for scripture by its peculiar claims to "bring to life" the narratives and characters of the canonical literature.

Perhaps more subtly, and certainly more enduringly, the literature of the west is saturated by the Bible as perhaps by no other single source. Northrop Frye once wrote:

> In European literature, down to the last couple of centuries, the myths of the Bible have formed a special category, as a body of stories with a distinctive authority. Poets who attach themselves to this central mythical area, like Dante or Milton, have been thought of as possessing a special kind of seriousness conferred on them by their subject matter.[36]

My intention is to shift the focus to precisely these last couple of centuries, and to examine the nature of the intertextuality between recent fiction and what Robert Alter has described as "the beginnings of prose fiction".[37] Fascination with the canon of scripture and its interpretation has continued, outside the specific concerns of the communities of the faithful, in the novels of Thomas Mann, Joseph Heller, Julian Barnes and many others. In what sense are these writers also authors of scripture within the traditions of the canon, affirming its stability and at the same time recognizing its adaptability?

Finally, some attention must be given to the contemporary phenomenon of apocalyptic in art, the cinema and literature. Why is our own time apparently so susceptible to a rebirth of the images and often their violence which are so firmly embedded in both testaments, in Daniel, in the gospels, and, perhaps above all, in the Book of Revelation? Maybe the very conclusion of the biblical canon, as finally established, with an apocalypse is significant as our own literary imagination is soaked in apocalyptic concern, the very shape of the canon's narrative subtly rehearsed not in the assumptions of a theologically driven *heilsgeschichte* but in the deep structures of our whole literary and artistic corpus, reflecting in our experience and culture the profound, often shadowy, impulse towards a theological perception as yet largely inarticulate and unrealized – certainly within those traditions of faith which would claim to be the guardians of theology and its referential claims.

The story, long begun, continues, the canonical disclosure necessarily without closure . . .

Notes

1. James A. Sanders, *Canon and Community: A Guide to Canonical Criticism* (Philadelphia, 1984) p. xv.
2. See, further, J. N. D. Kelly, *Early Christian Doctrines*, 4th edn (London, 1968) pp. 56ff.
3. See James A. Sanders, *From Sacred Story to Sacred Text: Canon as Paradigm* (Philadelphia, 1987) p. 181.
4. See René Girard, *Job: The Victim of His People* (London, 1987) p. 143.
5. See James G. Williams, *The Bible, Violence and the Sacred: Liberation from the Myth of Sanctioned Violence* (San Francisco, 1991) p. 176.
6. Rudolf Bultmann, *Theology of the New Testament*, vol. 2, trans. Kendrick Grobel (London, 1955) p. 141.
7. Elisabeth Schüssler Fiorenza, *In Memory of Her: A Feminist Theological Reconstruction of Christian Origins* (London, 1983) pp. 5–7.

8. Brevard S. Childs, *The New Testament as Canon: An Introduction* (Philadelphia, 1985) p. 15.
9. James A. Sanders, Foreword to Robert W. Wall and Eugene E. Lemcio, *The New Testament as Canon: A Reader in Canonical Criticism*, JSNT, Supplement Series 76 (Sheffield, 1992) p. 10.
10. See Ray L. Hart, *Unfinished Man and the Imagination: Toward an Ontology and a Rhetoric of Revelation* (Atlanta, 1985) pp. 37–8.
11. See Robert Morgan with John Barton, *Biblical Interpretation* (Oxford, 1988) pp. 213–14.
12. Brevard S. Childs, *Old Testament Theology in a Canonical Context* (London, 1985) p. 6.
13. Childs, *The New Testament as Canon*, p. 36.
14. Sanders, *Canon and Community*, p. 68.
15. C. F. D. Moule, *The Birth of the New Testament*, 2nd edn (London, 1966) p. 209.
16. Childs, *The New Testament as Canon*, p. 23.
17. Ibid., p. 13.
18. James A. Sanders, *Torah and Canon* (Philadelphia, 1972) p. 9.
19. Ibid., p. xv.
20. See Sanders, *From Sacred Story to Sacred Text*.
21. Childs, *The New Testament as Canon*, p. 136. Childs is referring specifically here to the work of Rudolf Bultmann, Ernst Käsemann and Wayne Meeks.
22. Sanders, *From Sacred Story to Sacred Text*, p. 5.
23. See further, Robert Detweiler, "After the New Criticism: Contemporary Methods of Literary Interpretation", in Richard A. Spencer (ed.), *Orientation by Disorientation: Studies in Literary Criticism and Biblical Literary Criticism* (Pittsburgh, 1980) pp. 9–10.
24. Paul de Man, *The Resistance to Theory* (Manchester, 1986) p. 11.
25. J. Hillis Miller, *The Ethics of Reading* (New York, 1987) p. 45.
26. Childs, *The New Testament as Canon*, Excursus III: "The Canonical Approach and the 'New Yale Theology'", pp. 541–6.
27. Ibid., p. 543.
28. George A. Lindbeck, *The Nature of Doctrine: Religion and Theology in a Postliberal Age* (London, 1984) pp. 113–24.
29. Childs, *The New Testament as Canon*, p. 540.
30. See, further, Stephen D. Moore, *Literary Criticism and the Gospels: The Theoretical Challenge* (New Haven and London, 1989) pp. 72–3; Lubomír Doložel, "Eco and His Model Reader", *Poetics Today*, 1 (1980) 181–8; Mark G. Brett, "The Future of Reader Criticisms?", in Francis Watson (ed.), *The Open Text: New Directions for Biblical Studies?* (London, 1993) p. 14.
31. See Morgan with Barton, *Biblical Interpretation*, p. 214.
32. Stephen D. Moore, "God's Own (Pri)son: the Disciplinary Technology of the Cross", in Watson, *The Open Text*, pp. 121–39.
33. Hart, *Unfinished Man*, p. 38.
34. Jan Gorak, *The Making of the Modern Canon: Genesis and Crisis of a Literary Idea* (London and Atlantic Highland, N.J., 1991) p. 1.
35. Childs, *The New Testament as Canon*, p. 41.

36. Northrop Frye, *The Secular Scripture: A Study of the Structure of Romance* (Cambridge, Mass., and London, 1976) p. 7; see also Northrop Frye, *The Double Vision: Language and Meaning in Religion* (Toronto, 1991).
37. Robert Alter, *The Art of Biblical Narrative* (London, 1981) ch. 2, pp. 23–46.

3

The Literary Classic and the Tragedy of Fiction

Alongside questions concerning the canon and canonicity, considerable critical attention has been given of late to the nature of the "classic" text in literature.[1] The uneasy relationship between the classic text and the notion of canon, in secular or sacred literature, has very much to do, I contest, with the relationship on the broader scale between literature and religion. The great classic texts of literature – indeed of all the arts – betray by their very nature an anxiety, an unsteadiness, an accidental quality. It is precisely this which distinguishes them from the conventional, the everyday and the commonplace. They exist uneasily in time, yet they survive precisely because of this quality which is their genius, unrepeatable and revelatory. The huge blasphemy of any claim to "reproduce" the classic text and deny its unique quality is expressed by Jorge Luis Borges's "Pierre Menard, Author of the *Quixote*": "The final term in a theological or metaphysical demonstration – the objective world, God, causality, the forms of the universe – is no less previous and common than my famed novel."[2] As David Tracy has put it, the accident of the classic becomes its destiny, its very flaws contributing to the greater whole.

The classic, unique work of literature, both in form and content, invites us to undertake the *risk* of reading it, always threatening the conventions which, perhaps, gave rise to it. As that supremely steady English critic of the eighteenth century, Dr Samuel Johnson, quaintly expressed it: "The essence of poetry is invention; such invention as, by producing something unexpected, surprises and delights. The topics of devotion are few, and being few are universally known; but, few as they are, they can be made no more."[3]

This intrinsic unsteadiness of the literary classic gives rise, in the field of religious literature, and above all the literature of the scriptural canon, to a profound, uncomfortable dialectic which it will be the canon's tendency to resolve. The theology of the devout interpreter will always seek to iron out the unfollowable world of literary genius. The author of Matthew's Gospel, one may suppose, was troubled enough by the wayward poetry of his predecessor in Mark's Gospel to straighten out many of his most mysterious moments. What one may call a "religious classic" – and Mark's Gospel is, finally, just that: a canonical work, though long-neglected – will always bear a paradigmatic claim to truth and reality. Yet this very Gospel is a trenchant example of a canonical work which *almost* escapes the bounds of its religious purpose. Why was it for so long neglected, and now has become almost an obsession with "literary" critics who have begun to turn their attention to scripture? The centuries of "misdoubt" which confined this work arise out of its very poetic strength – its *power*. Following Harold Bloom, I draw the word "misdoubt" from Andrew Marvell's poem "On Mr Milton's *Paradise Lost*":

> the Argument
> Held me a while misdoubting his Intent,
> That he would ruin (for I saw him strong)
> The sacred Truths to Fable and old Song . . .
> Yet as I read, soon growing less severe,
> I liked his project, the success did fear . . .
> That Majesty which through thy work doth reigh
> Draws the devout, deterring the profane.
> And things divine thou treatst of in such state
> As them preserves, and thee inviolate.
> (lines 5–8, 11–12, 31–4)[4]

This, the Milton whom Blake was to accuse of being "of the Devil's party". As with all "strong" poets, even perhaps the author of Mark's Gospel, we tend to perceive in his genius the ruin of sacred *truths* as they are appropriated anew, scandalously. Yet, finally, this very strength may, paradoxically, be a preservative, though always uneasy. Such works as this Gospel, or the poems of the Christian Milton (note I do not say the Christian poems of Milton), walk a delicate tightrope between truth and power – interpreters beware, for the risk of reading is great.

Although a first drafting or formal recognition of a fixed canon of New Testament writings cannot be dated before Marcion in the middle of the second century CE, it is clear that from the very start the New Testament writers were aware of the need to establish the particular authority of their books from among others already available. Certain books claim to stand out from among the many. The writer of Luke's Gospel, for example, admits in his opening words to Theophilus, that "inasmuch as many have undertaken to compile a narrative of the things which have been accomplished among us . . . it seemed good to me also . . . that you may know the truth concerning the things of which you have been informed" (1: 1–4). The intention, then, is to guide the reader in the way of truth, perplexed as he seems to be by a multiplicity of versions and stories. As the "canon" of scripture began to evolve and become authoritatively established in the early Christian Church, it quickly became necessary to isolate the "genuine" from the spurious or apocryphal writings. In the second century CE, Irenaeus argues that "it is not possible that the Gospels can be either more or fewer in number than they are":

> For, since there are four zones of the world in which we live, and four principal winds, while the church has been scattered throughout all the world, and the "pillar and ground" of the church is the gospel and the spirit of life; it is fitting that she should have four pillars, breathing incorruption on every side, and vivifying men afresh.[5]

The task of establishing the canonical authority of the four gospels was urgent as apocryphal gospels proliferated – Irenaeus points out that a so-called "Gospel of Truth" had recently been composed – and those outside the Church perceived disagreement rather than coherence in the truth among believers. A little later than Irenaeus, Origen defends the four evangelists against their spurious rivals inasmuch as only they had received the necessary gifts of grace for their task. Origen rejects such works as the Gospels of Peter, Thomas and Matthias on the grounds that

> the thought and purport of their contents is so absolutely out of harmony with true orthodoxy, as to establish the fact that they are certainly the forgeries of heretics. For this reason they ought not even to be placed among the spurious writings, but refused as altogether monstrous and impious.[6]

The argument for the origin of the scriptural canon as emerging from divine initiative – a gift of grace – is difficult either to entertain or reject in academic discussion, though it continues from Origen to the biblical scholarship of the present day. What, however, concerns me more here is Origen's argument for canonicity from within the confines of a perceived theological orthodoxy. How quickly in the history of Christianity do the canons of the Church come to define and regulate the canon of scripture, and therefore the status of the texts within that canon! As Frank Kermode freely admits, defences of the literature of the New Testament are bound to be subject to "interested inquiry", selecting from Friedrich Schleiermacher the remark that "a continuing preoccupation with the New Testament canon which was not motivated by one's own interest in Christianity can only be directed against the canon".[7]

The danger in this legitimate recognition is that the canon may so easily become merely the instrument of ecclesial interest, not only simply reinforcing its theological assumptions, but reflecting passively its exclusive ethos and ideology. From the earliest days of Christianity the irony threatens whereby the Church defines scripture, rather than scripture promoting the Church, its beliefs and practices. The canon becomes, thereby, an instrument of principled, systematic exclusion in a dangerous game of power politics – or, at least, this becomes a grave danger as individual texts come to be "read" only within the boundaries of canonical orthodoxy whose "sacred truth" is thereby defended, inviolate. Within this game of power politics, strong "classic" texts will tend to become tamed by their acceptance into the canon – so that, paradoxically, the Church has become generally a very bad "reader" of scripture, and in particular of those tests within scripture whose literary status is most energetic and, perhaps, perplexing. The power of canonical authority simply veils the energy of textual "literality". This fatal flaw reveals, it seems to me, a more, general fatal flaw for theology today in its failure to recognize the tragic defeat in the cultural domain of truth by power.[8] If, indeed, the canon does in the end operate as a powerful instrument of systematic exclusion, then one might be obliged to recognize there the principle that power fears not so much the truth, as other agencies of power. There is, indeed, nothing so threatening to the canon as the strong "classic" text of literature – which the canon will tend to try and appropriate. Traditionally the canon of scripture, it might be said, has been regarded as the container of conclusive wisdom, the passive reflector of a particular ethos, theology or ideology, to which nothing may be added and from which nothing may be taken away. As Dr Johnson expressed it, "omnipotence cannot be exalted; infinity be amplified; perfection cannot be improved". But may we not rather perceive the canon of scripture as a record of communities' struggles, *in their contexts*, with issues of faith and belief? The canonical paradigm, as James Sanders might put it, shows how believing communities might claim to hear the voice of God from outside the inner community traditions.[9] There is, then properly, a note of anxious enquiry, a sense of risk necessarily within canonical texts, for these are texts with the strength and power to survive through change and under stress. Such texts will also, in a way, be classics – their canonicity a result of their very unease within the canon. That is part of the paradox that, in order to remain true to our identity, we must be prepared to change.

There is, and always has been, a problem and an instability surrounding the task of biblical interpretation, a problem which may be summed up in the tension between the recognition of the books of the Bible as, on the one hand, literature and, on the other hand, what T. S. Eliot called "the report of the Word of God".[10] One recent book with the title *The Bible as Literature* devoutly, in its turn, expresses the dilemma:

> Although the writing of the Bible may well have been under divine inspiration and although it may be regarded in its entirely as God's revelation, God did not put a single word of it on paper. . . . The writing of the Bible was done by human beings, acting in history – in human history.[11]

Critically this is less than honest, for it disallows a particular kind of reading – anything which is less (or more) than orthodox or "authoritative". This same book continues to describe the scriptural canon as "the list of genuine and authoritative books that make up the only proper contents of the Bible".

Now is this, or is this not, the way to describe the great classical texts of literature from Homer, Aeschylus to the present day? The answer is both "yes" and "no", for while the canon is ultimately plural but determinate, the classic text by contrast, is essentially singular but indeterminate. The literary critic Paul de Man, in his 1979 essay "Shelley Disfigured",[12] regards the process of canonization negatively as a self-serving desire to repair the ruins of time, a desire he describes as "monumentalization", which involves submerging the overwhelming contingency of the literary text in what he calls "monstrously predictable" interpretations governed by impulses to circumscription and definition.

But, on the other hand, what constitutes the authority of the classic of literature? It seems to me to be closely connected with the notions of time and the sacred. For if a canon serves to repair the ruins of time, there must also be that in it which will not run parallel with it, but will actually open up a point of purchase on it. Equally, if the canon serves to preserve sacred truth "inviolate", it will only effectively do so by making it its own – by, in other words, effecting its ruin. There is that intrinsic authority in the classic which constitutes the scandal (to use St Paul's word) of history – the human medium, and the sacred – the divine medium, and draws them together. There must, therefore, always be a note of the uncanonical in the canon – that element of the literary which, as Coleridge describes the "secondary imagination" in *Biographia Literaria* (1817), always uncomfortably "dissolves, diffuses, dissipates, in order to recreate".

It was the poet Coleridge again in his late, theological work *Aids to Reflection* (1828), who wrote: "He who begins by loving Christianity better than Truth, will proceed by loving his own sect or church better than Christianity, and end in loving himself better than all." Any notion of truth guarded by canonical authority which finally merely sustains the continuity of an institution – whether it be Israel, Christianity or the Church – will ultimately tend to collapse inwards. Coleridge's aphorism demonstrates one version of the tragic defeat of truth by power, and this note of tragedy will tend to sound when the poetics of the literary begin to prise open the systematics of the canon. One becomes conscious then of the element of discontinuity in continuity, in Paul Ricoeur's phrase of reorientation by disorientation – a recognition that if the mysterious power of a genuine, human insight is not acknowledged, then the tyranny of "monumentalization" will ensue.

As an illustration of the way in which literature, and the literary classic, must always be recognized in the reading of the religious canon of the Bible, I turn now to a number of retellings of biblical narratives in modern fictional writings – works which may or may not be claimed as "classics", yet remain insistently and overwhelmingly "literary".

In his immensely influential essay entitled "Odysseus' Scar"[13] Erich Auerbach examines in detail the literary qualities of the Akedah, the story of the sacrifice of Isaac in Genesis 22. Auerbach demonstrates how the focus and distance of the narrative alters as the story progresses and reaches its climax. Like a camera with a zoom lens, the description begins with a wide, general sweep through the journey to the land of Moriah to the sharper detail, closer and closer, of the impending sacrifice, to the crucial moment in verse 10 which describes in detail Abraham's two actions: "Then Abraham put forth his hand, and took the knife to slay his son."

What Auerbach argues is that the literary pace, perspective and focus of the story of Isaac's sacrifice is dedicated to a specific purpose – that is to demonstrate the activity and purposes of God for Abraham, the story of the divine test, which Abraham passes with flying colours. (I discuss different readings of the narrative in the next chapter, using, among others, Woody Allen and Rembrandt.) Leaving for now the notorious interpretational problems of this passage, my suggestion here is that in modern fictional rehearsals of Old Testament stories we find these familiar narratives presented from perspectives other than that of the history of God's purpose for his people. They become no longer the patriarchal narratives of God's elect and chosen – Moses the lawgiver, Samson the judge, David the King of messianic proportions – but stories of individuals and families trapped in a theological vision, usually its victims or slaves, and most often tragically experiencing what Elaine Scarry has called the conversion of real pain into the fiction of power.[14] I contend that, although there is an element of comedy in this process, the primary note of these "fictions" is tragic, a reflection of the contemporary tragedy of theology and possibly sounding a literary note of hope for it.

In his well-known book entitled *The Art of Biblical Narrative*, the American Jewish scholar Robert Alter offers what he describes as a literary approach to the Bible, which is, for him, the Old Testament. His contention is a simple one – that literary art plays a crucial role in the shaping of biblical narrative, in a series of careful and detailed literary analyses of familiar passages such as Genesis 38, the story of Tamar and her father-in-law Judah. Treating these figures as one might scrutinize the characters in a novel or fictional narrative, Alter claims a theological purpose. Thus, he contends:

> What we need to understand better is that the religious vision of the Bible is given depth and subtlety precisely by being conveyed through the most sophisticated resources of prose fiction . . . Almost the whole range of biblical narrative . . . embodies the basic perception that man must live before God, in the transforming medium of time, incessantly and perplexingly in relation with others.[15]

Robert Alter remains devoutly within the religious purposes of scripture, and his work is, undoubtedly, extremely illuminating in many ways.

But what happens when we take these narratives out of that context, turning the focus of the camera lens slightly so that these men and women come to us with different preoccupations perhaps religious but, as with most of us, their religion confusingly involved in other experiences of power, love, pain, hatred, longing. One notorious recent instance of this in the critical world is Harold Bloom's commentary on the, so-called, *Book of J*, extracted from the "Jahwistic" strands of the pentateuchal narratives: that is, what are perceived as the earliest elements, revised or censored by the E ("Elohist"), P ("Priestly") and D ("Deuteronomic") strands.[16] How serious, or ironic, Bloom intends to be I am not sure (is he, indeed, writing "fiction"?) – though that in itself is profoundly significant – when he proposes that the author of these scriptural writings is a sophisticated lady of aristocratic preferences with a penchant for irony, her natural successor in the history of Jewish literature being Franz Kafka. Neither a theologian, nor a deliberate historian of the religious history of the Jewish people, this lady is a literary genius anticipating the writings of Aeschylus, Shakespeare, Tolstoy and the canon of *secular* literature in our experience. Quite unlike Robert Alter, Harold Bloom suggests that:

> Recovering J will *not* throw new light on Torah or on the Hebrew Bible or on the Bible of Christianity. I do *not* think that appreciating J will help us love God or arrive at the spiritual or historical truth of whatever Bible. I want the varnish off because it conceals a writer of the eminence of Shakespeare or Dante, and such a writer is worth more than many creeds, many churches, many scholarly certainties. (p. 44, my emphases)

Now this begs many questions. Alter seeks to recover what the scriptural narratives "mean to tell us about God, man, and the perilously momentous realm of history".[17] Even if we accept that this is a great deal more significant than the business of creeds, churches and scholarly certainties, in what sense is Bloom claiming *more* than Alter? What actually constitutes the literary "eminence" which he attributes to his aristocratic, curiously postmodern, genius?

Bloom's game is, of course, "literary" rather than "theological", at least in the first instance. "What happens", he asks, "to representation when altogether incommensurate realities juxtapose and clash?" Abandon the theological basis of the scriptural canon, and what does it signify when a narrative draws together in one dramatic encounter an Abraham with a Yahweh, or a Jacob with a nameless one among the Elohim? This is how one standard biblical commentary describes I and II Samuel:

> Samuel and David, who make a frame round the dark, problematical figure of King Saul, are figures of striking significance in this history of the kingdom, and much of the message of the Bible is embodied in their lives and in their struggles; and all three, each in his own way, are forerunners and heralds of the real King.[18]

The story in the theological discussion of this commentator is not really about these three characters, who have merely "striking significance", merely embody a message, and are without genuine human status in the shadow of the "real" King. But what if we make the story about them as feeling, suffering people – and what then of that incommensurate reality, God himself? Here one begins to perceive a role for the ironist – uneasy, troubled by the role left for theology in the history of salvation. Thus changing the focus and perspective of our reading we begin to feel Bloom's point when he remarks that

> J's attitude towards Yahweh resembles nothing so much as a mother's somewhat wary but still proudly amused stance towards a favourite son who has grown up to be benignly powerful but also eccentrically irascible. Such a stance feels ironic, but again, how are we to categorize such an irony? (pp. 24–5)

In Bloom's commentary, God himself becomes a character in the story alongside the human figures, and the careful theological separation of levels of reality which reduces men to mere embodiments of agents of the biblical message is confused. What, then, does theology do? Even more, we can assemble in the literary drama other figures who are reduced to a still lower level than the great men who are kings and heroes. What of those women without a political or religious role in canonically sanctioned salvation history? Focus upon their pathetic or tragic dramas, and how does the God of history respond?

Here is one example. It is all too easy to overlook the dreadful story in Judges 19 of the young woman exposed by her husband to gang-rape. To avoid the "outrage" of buggery, the woman is offered as a substitute for the man: "the Levite took hold of his concubine and thrust her outside for them. They assaulted her and abused her all night till the morning, and when dawn broke, they let her go. . . . he picked up a knife, and he took hold of his concubine and cut her up limb by limb into twelve pieces; and he sent them through the length and breadth of Israel" (Judges 19: 25, 29). Peake's standard one-volume commentary barely mentions the woman at all – noting only the "wickedness . . . perpetrated against a man who was both a Levite and a sojourner".[19]

Theology, and a view of "salvation" history, has simply written out this terrible story – thus history constructs itself, and its tool is thematization.[20]

Against this canonical obsession with salvation history may we not have a right, then, to introduce into our reading the discourses of fiction to allow their different levels full interplay and to plead the human case of a forgotten woman so treated in the pages of sacred scripture? Rather than dominance or subservience, may we not seek the possibility of mutual illumination? Just as official religion has grown too accustomed to using texts as instruments of violation, so one may have to take the risk of living life textually and not according to the sanitized glamour of the institutional history of religion. The novelists whom I will come to in a moment have, I suggest, become adept at listening to what the text had to say by picking up the recalcitrant details that biblical scholars and "official" readings of scripture have problems with. Moving from "holy writ" to "wholly writ", as Mieke Bal has put it, the modes available for the story in Judges 19 "in our present culture would be either pornography or high symbolism".[21] We have to ask which is the moral choice.

In 1989, the English novelist Julian Barnes published a fiction entitled *A History of the World in 10½ Chapters*. The first chapter begins on a note of high comedy. It is a re-telling of the familiar story of Noah's ark from Genesis 6–8, told by, it seems, one of the animals on board. The magisterial biblical narrator confidently places the story within the theme of the covenant between God and Noah, who was, we are assured, "a righteous man, the one blameless man of his time; he walked with God" (Genesis 6: 9). The scriptural discussion between God and Noah before the flood did not, of course, involve any of the animals. The narrator in Barnes's "history" notes this "political" exclusion with some bitterness:

> As far as we were concerned the whole business of the Voyage began when we were invited to report to a certain place by a certain time. That was the first we heard of the scheme. We didn't know anything of the political background. God's wrath with his own creation was news to us; we just got caught up in it willy-nilly.[22]

But if the animals on the Ark are altogether excluded from the politics of God's plan, neither is Noah's place in the history of salvation and its theology self-evident. The anonymous narrator continues:

> I suppose it wasn't altogether Noah's fault. I mean, that God of his was a really oppressive role-model. Noah couldn't do anything without first wondering what He would think. Now that's no way to go on. Always looking over your shoulder for approval – it's not adult, is it? Noah didn't have the excuse of being a young man either . . . There was something a bit sinister about Noah's devotion to God; creepy, if you know what I mean. (p. 21)

Well, of course, we do know what he means. From the outside, the theological justification for the episode of the flood threatens to seem high comedy.

And yet Barnes's narrator is intensely serious, his perspective effectively deconstructing the biblical justification of Noah. In the Genesis narrative, Noah is told by the Lord that he alone is righteous before him in his generation (7: 1). But it does not seem that way to at least one animal on board the Ark. Which animal tells the story in Barnes's "history"? Only in the very last sentence do we learn that it is, in fact, . . . a woodworm; on a wooden ship? A stowaway, of course, for Noah would not have deliberately taken the risk of entertaining such a natural deconstructor of his vessel. Nor, presumably, would his theology have risked so much.

Comedy, if not so bitter, has always been an element in the "fictional" rehearsal of scripture. The literature and drama of the Middle Ages abound in comic retellings of biblical stories. But in Barnes a particular note of theological misalignment is sounded, leaving one uneasy yet amused. More common than this in modern fictional retellings of the Old Testament, however, is the note of tragedy. In his Foreword to the vast four-volume work *Joseph und Seine Brüder*, Thomas Mann repeatedly affirms the book's "comedy", its "humanization" of the biblical narratives and its assertion of "that fellow feeling for which mankind has always been sensitively receptive",[23] yet throughout the work is the dark recognition of its conception against the tragic background of Mann's Europe from which he fled to America, his return home impossible. Reflecting deeply upon the Bible story, he develops the figure of Tamar, "the daughter-in-law and seductress of Judah, whom I made into Jacob's pupil, an Astarte-like figure, endowed, at the same time, with features from the Book of Ruth" (p. xii). Let Tamar, for one instant, be our insight into Mann's vast literary achievement.

Robert Alter in his close critical reading of Tamar's story in Genesis 38 claims that the student of the Bible has more to learn from his literary approach than from modern biblical scholarship,[24] and he notes similarities between his own reading and ancient Jewish midrash. But the modern reader, I suggest, would find everything proposed so triumphantly by Alter – and now often quoted in textbooks – already in Mann's fiction: the close parallels with the Joseph story, the intertextuality, the sheer narrative energy. And there is more in the novel, for here Tamar also becomes a woman, an individual, and a figure of dark tragedy:

> and there for ever remains the story of the woman who would not at any price let herself be put aside, but with astounding tenacity wormed herself into a place in the line of descent. There she stands, tall and almost sinister, on the slope of her native hills; one hand on her body, the other shading her eyes, she looks out upon the fruitful plains where the light breaks from towering clouds to radiate in waves of glory across the land. (p. 1042)

Like Rembrandt (as we shall see in the next chapter), and unlike Robert Alter, Mann pierces through the theological configuration of our readings of Genesis 38 to the humanity within the story, and to its tragic dimensions.

Mann's novel owes much to his exile to America, and to the hills of California. Joseph Heller's *God Knows* (1984), on the other hand, is a product of brash, chattering New York. An "autobiography" of King David, *God Knows* follows closely the narratives of the first and second Books of Samuel and the first two chapters of I Kings. It is far from being scurrilous, though often very funny, full of sex, bad language and what the narrator David calls "exciting chase scenes".

From the start he enjoys a talkative relationship with God, while maintaining a healthily sceptical attitude towards the laws given to Moses "that did not make things easier for us". At once modern and ancient David lives lustily, scornful of other "heroes" of Israelite history – "Samson, that goon, that troglodyte, that hairy ape." The great and miraculous stories of his rise to power, like the slaying of Goliath against all the odds, are reduced by his native cunning and insight into the obvious; sling the stone and run like mad: "Goliath didn't stand a chance. The poor fucker was a goner. With either hand, every one of those chosen men of Benjamin could sling stones at a hairbreadth fifty yards away and never miss." David, the cocky Jewish lad, the cunning guerrilla fighter, the increasingly overburdened King, plays his part with panache, but his very military and political success brings its own human tragedy. Quite simply, how, as a lusty human being, can he cope with being God's chosen and anointed King? How can he sustain the configurations of the biblical *heilgeschichte*, the salvation history of Israel?

King David's speech to Solomon, his heir, in I Kings 2, is a devastatingly controlled example of politico-theological rhetoric. "Fulfil your duty to the Lord your God", he says to his son, "conform to his ways, observe his statutes and his commandments . . . so that you may prosper in whatever you do" (I Kings 2: 3). Religious history is kept intact, but at what human cost? Heller's David is more honest and pragmatic. He admits that his final speech is an act, and a duty, and it is at least much better than other "canonical" examples of deathbed speeches in the history of Israelite religion:

> My farewell address was a much better one than Jacob's on his deathbed, which was inappropriate as a blessing and almost incomprehensible in content and objective. . . . The speech I gave at least was functional.[25]

As King and instrument of God's purpose, David continues to "function": but as an ageing, decaying human being, he has lost that first fine glory of interaction with the God of Israel. And so, the book ends on a note approaching the tragic – the tragedy of an old man:

> You think I am at peace now with my Maker? Anything but. I am thinking of God now, and I am thinking of Saul. I think of Saul in his wordless gloom and torment every time I came to his chamber to play for him, and I realize as I remember that I never saw a sadder face on human being until a little while ago, when Abishag the Shunamnite held up a mirror for me to see and I looked at mine. . . . I want my God back; and they send me a girl. (pp. 446–7)

But who is this God upon whom David so devoutly calls? Not the God of scripture, for he has died (as Nietzsche proclaimed) or disappeared? God knows.

Torgny Lindgren's version of the Davidic story in his novel *Bathsheba* (1984) is, by comparison with Heller, cold, stark and nordic. Here, at the end, the narrator is Bathsheba herself, and David's tragedy is also God's tragedy – again both trapped in the solemn cadences of salvation history. David experiences, not the disappearance of God, but the inescapability of God, for, in a sense, he and God are one in a cruel theology. "The Lord is always present. You can see that He is with me now. Whatever I do, I can never free myself from Him – He is all around me. . . . When one is forsaken by Him, one realizes how real He is."[26] Finally, Bathsheba cannot distinguish between God and his servant, the anointed King:

> The temple servants carry him; his palanquin is like the ark of the Lord, and he sits beneath the wings of the cherubim. Yes, I am speaking of King David. (p. 240)

In death, holiness no longer helps him, but his joy in Bathsheba has the coldness of his love for God: for, to David, she is perfection – and her perfection is her greatest flaw.

The terrible flaw of tragedy permeates these contemporary perspectives on the scriptural narrative. My final fictional example in this chapter takes us back to Genesis, and the brief story of Cain and Abel in Chapter 4. Moelwyn Merchant's short monologue entitled "Cain makes his plea", published in a collection of four biblical narratives under the title *Inherit the Land* (1992), follows a poetic fascination in English literature, most notably in Lord Byron and S. T. Coleridge, with the tragic figure of Cain. Once again, the confident biblical note of the Lord's presence is here muted in Cain's human cry of desolation making its just, confused plea to God:

> But Lord! Listen to my cry, Lord! Mine was the sacrifice. That acrid smoke was the sweat of my face and arms! Those flames were reluctant to turn to ash the grain for which I had so bitterly laboured! Do you wonder, Lord, that my heart ached as the sheaves were consumed. I denied you nothing, Lord, grudged you nothing . . .[27]

One feels in Cain's desperate protest that powerful sense of the ineluctable progress of the purposes of the biblical God – the theodical problem which John Milton struggled with in *Paradise Lost*, of justifying God's ways to men, in the face of the tragedy of human weakness, misery, and the genuine desire to do a best which never seems to be good enough.

For, in Merchant's prose, Cain approaches truly tragic proportions. Not the rough, callous murderer of our tradition, he is sensitive to the forbidden beauty of Eden, a committed worker, a man of dreams. He cries, with perhaps prospective irony:

> Lord God! Can you, in your remote majesty, imagine desolation? Can you begin to know the dereliction I have known, despised, rejected, cast out? Can suffering touch your heart, Lord? (p. 4)

Merchant clearly has in mind the later "Christian" story, but for *Cain* a silence from God would evoke the response of the literary critic William Empson in his formidable and angry classic of Milton studies, *Milton's God*:

> The root of his [Milton's] power is that he could accept and express a downright horrible conception of God and yet keep somehow alive, underneath it, all the breadth and generosity, the welcome to every noble pleasure, which had been prominent in European history just before his time.[28]

Now what preserves Thomas Mann, Julian Barnes, Joseph Heller and other writers of fiction from concluding with Empson that the

God, first encountered in our literary inheritance in the pages of the Jewish Bible, is simply horrible? Their modern "novels" have turned the perspective of scripture to the confused and vulnerable experience of the human participants in the stories, and made it tragic. In his early work *The Death of Tragedy*, George Steiner begins with the assertion that tragedy is alien to the Judaic sense of the world. Job, perhaps the closest to a tragic vision in the Bible, stands on the periphery of Judaism, and even here, Steiner asserts, "an orthodox hand has asserted the claims of justice against those of tragedy".[29] Orthodoxy and the hand of canonical authority mask the pain of tragedy, while the spirit of Judaism is vehement in its conviction that the order of the universe and of man's estate is, finally, accessible to reason, even in the face of Jehovah's fury.

But does it *seem* so to David, or Cain – or the miserable animals on the ark? For them the business of salvation history can only be perceived within the paradoxes of incommensurate realities – the human and the divine, only within the *individuality* of their respective sufferings, or even their comic vision.

And the recovery of a tragic vision is, I suggest, necessary. Literature, then, offers to the Bible neither a bland theology, nor a meaningless ordeal, but individual catastrophes and a lived experience which provides no answers, but sustains a perverse longing for God which is hard to understand: "I want my God back; and they send me a girl"; "your perfection is your greatest flaw"; "why was I, Cain, made to have these longings and never to know the truths?". The voices speak from the narratives – utterances of pain in a literature that frets within the canon which yet preserves it.

Joseph Heller's King David is not impious: he merely admits that he cannot sustain the role which the theology of canonical scripture imposes upon him. The timelessness of human experience, expressed in the tragic singularity of literature (David joins the other great, unique, lonely figures of literature from Ulysses to Oedipus, Lear and even Madame Bovary) here overcomes the constructed continuity of the temporal flow of the scriptural history of salvation. In the event, both he – and God – are stupid. Here is exactly the pattern of Milton's *Paradise Lost*, a most profound religious vision, though in it, on literary grounds, the great hero is Satan.

So, I suspect, it must always be, as literature and its classics expose that delicate, absurd and ultimately tragic scriptural balance between truth and power. This tension is neatly expressed by T. S. Eliot in his 1935 essay "Religion and Literature", and I see his point now, though it long offended me (and I cannot feel much sympathy with Eliot's underlying religious purpose):

> the Bible has had a *literary* influence upon English Literature *not* because it has been considered as literature, but because it has been considered as the report of the Word of God. And the fact that men of letters now discuss it as "literature" probably indicates the *end* of its "literary" influence.

Becoming a tragic, literary figure, David ceases to glow with messianic splendour as the instrument of Yahweh found in the canon of scripture. And yet, within the books of the canon there remains, as part of their very canonicity, that impulse to ruin the sacred "truths" of which they are the guardians. David Tracy makes the point that the religious classic specifically "will involve a claim to truth as the event of a disclosure – concealment of the whole of reality *by the power of the whole* – as, in some sense, a radical and finally gracious mystery".[30] Now it is this *power of the whole* which may make available in Scripture these *truth* claims which constitute their normative character as a religious text – but, I suspect that this very textual mystery is also prompted by a literariness which is perverse, riddling, deconstructive, oddly constructed, somehow ill-matched. If the great classics of literature were simply continuous with expectations of normativity or convention, they would cease to be classics: and the great literary works of the Bible – the Genesis narratives, the Song of Songs, the Book of Job, Mark's Gospel, the Apocalypse – are beautifully yet profoundly uneasily constructed wholes. They dissolve and dissipate in order to recreate. They at once invite and subvert canonical reading, and the subversion is revealed in the tragedy and comedy of the literary re-tellings with which this chapter has been concerned.

One must, then, acknowledge the dialectical character in the literature of the canon, between, perhaps, literature and theology. Even as we believe, we are left uneasy by Mark's Gospel – as clearly was the author of Matthew – or by the edgy rhetoric of Paul's epistles – and how they have lent themselves to powerful misuse in the history of the Church! The fragmented obscurity of their narratives is part of their mystery, and why do we, guiltily, continue to read them as classics of literature – yet unlike other literature?

What, finally, is the mysterious relationship between truth and power in the terms of my discussion? Our fear must be that, loving our religion as the truth, we come to love it in preference to the truth: salvation lies in the recognition that scripture, the guardian of the truth of religion, is also text, partaking of the healthy scepticism of literature and its classics. The tragic defeat of truth by power arises out of the fashionable Nietzschean surmise that truth and power are antithetical, or at least that truth can in every case be reduced to power. But replace antithesis with dialectic (or even dialogic), and one perceives that the classic is at once text and scripture, as scripture is at once text and classic. Yet, the terms must never be confused, for their distinction is the basis of their discontinuity within continuity. Michel Foucault puts it most succinctly:

> It's not a matter of emancipating truth from every system of power (which would be a chimera, for truth is already power) but of detaching the power of the truth from the forms of hegemony, social, economic [. . .] cultural [and, one might add, religious], within which it operates. . . .[31]

So literature, and its classics, must continue to trouble both the canon and its theology, from within and without, denying it the dangerous claims of communing directly with the Almighty.[32] Harold Bloom refers in his book *The Anxiety of Influence* (1973) to the figure of the Covering Cherub: in Genesis the cherub is God's Angel standing at the barred gate of Eden, in the poet Blake he is the Spectre of Milton, in Yeats the Spectre of Blake. In each case, the cherub is the figure which blocks the entrance to Paradise – that huge, authoritative anxiety which prevents creativeness and self-discovery. He is that which stifles creativity by the terrible weight of past genius. This demon of continuity and Spectre of canonical submission must be ousted in favour of the prophetic freedom of discontinuity which makes all things new – the truly unexpected fulfilment of that which has always been known.

And after all this, what finally do you want to make of Joseph Heller's David summing up his relationship with God, given David's role in scripture? Is it not very similar to what Milton came up with in his poem – perhaps inevitably and *rightly*? An advance on Nietzsche?!

. . . and I've got this ongoing, open-ended Mexican standoff with God, even though He might now be dead. Whether God is dead or not hardly matters, for we would use Him no differently anyway. He owes me an apology, but God won't budge so I won't budge. I have my faults, God knows, and I may even be among the first to admit them, but to this very day I know in my bones that I'm a much better person than He is.

Although I never actually *walked* with God, I did talk with Him a lot and got along with Him in perfect rapport until I offended Him for the first time; then He offended me, and later we offended each other. Even then he promised to protect me. And he has. (p. 14)

Notes

1. See, for example: T. S. Eliot, "What is a Classic?", in *Selected Prose of T. S. Eliot*, ed. Frank Kermode (New York, 1975) pp. 115–32. In response to this, Frank Kermode, *The Classic* (New York, 1975). For a selection of critical texts, see W. J. Bate (ed.), *Criticism: The Major Texts* (New York, 1970). For a more theological discussion, see David Tracy, *The Analogical Imagination: Christian Theology and the Culture of Pluralism* (London, 1981), esp. Part II: "Interpreting the Christian Classic".
2. Jorge Luis Borges, *Labyrinths: Selected Stories and Other Writings*, ed. Donald A. Yates and James E. Irby (Harmondsworth, 1981) p. 66.
3. Samuel Johnson, *Lives of the Poets* (1779–81), vol. I (Oxford, 1955) p. 203.
4. See Harold Bloom, *Ruin the Sacred Truths: Poetry and Belief from the Bible to the Present* (Cambridge, Mass., and London, 1989) p. 125.
5. Irenaeus, in J. Stevenson (ed.), *A New Eusebius* (London, 1960) p. 122.
6. Origen, in ibid., pp. 339–40.
7. Frank Kermode, "The Canon", in R. Alter and F. Kermode (eds), *The Literary Guide to the Bible* (London, 1987) p. 608.
8. See, further, David E. Klemm, "Back to Literature – and Theology?", in David Jasper (ed.), *Postmodernism, Literature and the Future of Theology* (London, 1993) pp. 180–90.
9. James A. Sanders, *Canon and Community* (Philadelphia, 1984) pp. 67–8.
10. T. S. Eliot, "Religion and Literature", in *Selected Essays*, 3rd edn (London, 1951) p. 390.
11. John B. Gabel and Charles B. Wheeler, *The Bible as Literature: An Introduction* (Oxford, 1986) p. 70.
12. Paul de Man, "Shelley Disfigured", in *Deconstruction and Criticism* (New York, 1979) pp. 39–73.

13. Erich Auerbach, *Mimesis: The Representation of Reality in Western Literature* (1946; trans. Willard R. Trask, Princeton, 1968) pp. 3–23.
14. Elaine Scarry, *The Body in Pain: The Making and Unmaking of the World* (Oxford, 1985).
15. Robert Alter, *The Art of Biblical Narrative* (London, 1981) p. 22.
16. See *The Book of J*, trans. David Rosenberg, interpreted Harold Bloom (London, 1991) pp. 3–5.
17. Alter, *Art of Biblical Narrative*, p. 189.
18. H. W. Hertzberg, *I and II Samuel: A Commentary*, trans. J. S. Bowden, The Old Testament Library (London, 1964) p. 20.
19. *Peake's Commentary on the Bible*, ed. Matthew Black and H. H. Rowley (London, 1962) pp. 314–15.
20. For a detailed account of this episode, see Mieke Bal, *Death and Dissymetry: The Politics of Coherence in the Book of Judges* (Chicago and London, 1988) *passim*, esp. pp. 119ff.
21. Ibid., p. 187. See also my review of *Death and Dissymetry*, in *Literature and Theology*, vol. 5 (1991) 327–8.
22. Julian Barnes, *A History of the World in 10½ Chapters* (London, 1989) p. 6.
23. Thomas Mann, *Joseph and His Brothers*, trans. H. T. Lowe-Porter (Harmondsworth, 1978) p. xiv.
24. Alter, *Art of Biblical Narrative*, pp. 5–12.
25. Joseph Heller, *God Knows* (1984; Black Swan, 1985) p. 443.
26. Torgny Lindgren, *Bathsheba*, trans. Tom Geddes (London, 1989) p. 90.
27. Moelwyn Merchant, *Inherit the Land* (Llandysul, 1992) p. 10.
28. William Empson, *Milton's God* (1961; Cambridge, 1981) pp. 276–7.
29. George Steiner, *The Death of Tragedy* (London, 1963) p. 4
30. David Tracy, "Creativity in the Interpretation of Religion: the Question of Radical Pluralism", *New Literary History*, vol. 15 (1983–4) 296.
31. Michel Foucault, "Truth and Power", in *Power/Knowledge: Selected Interviews and Other Writings, 1972–1977*, English trans. ed. Colin Gordon (New York, 1980) p. 133.
32. This sly phrase is taken from J. G. Ballard's short story "The Life and Death of God", in *Low-Flying Aircraft* (London, 1985) p. 143.

4

Seeing Pictures: Reading Texts

It should be clear by now that one of the underlying themes of this study is the way in which the canon may act to reinforce certain assumptions – religious, racial, sexual and so on. Texts within the canon may come to be read as supportive of such assumptions as controls, though other readings remain possible, readings against the grain of canonical demands. In this chapter I will deal largely, though not exclusively, with ways in which visual art has "read" the Bible, and in particular has drawn our attention to the bodies, literally the flesh and blood, of participants in and victims of the scriptural narratives. From a Christian religion which celebrates the word made flesh we return with some unease to the violated and discarded bodies in the canon of salvation history.

In *The History of Sexuality*, Michel Foucault demonstrates the close link between religion and sexuality. He writes:

> Today it is sex that serves as a support for the ancient form – so familiar and important in the West – of preaching. A great sexual sermon – which has had its subtle theologians and its popular voices – has swept through our societies over the last decades.[1]

Specifically, Foucault draws the link between modern sexual repression, power and knowledge. The exercise of power is almost inevitably repressive, and nowhere more effectively than in the control of our bodies and their sexuality. That which is "natural" is carefully defined – useless energies repressed, the efficient promotion of the social order commended in the structures of the family – and that which is "unnatural" is excluded. We "other Victorians" (to use Foucault's phrase), participate in a discourse of propriety which is designed to control our bodies, a discourse frequently validated by our religious tradition and its notions of canonicity. It is a moral discourse which, furthermore, tends to emphasize the distinction between the public and the private, and to sanction everything in terms of the former. Foucault expresses its power in this way:

> An imperative was established: Not only will you confess to acts contravening the law, but you will seek to transform your desire, your every desire, into discourse. Insofar as possible, nothing was meant to elude this dictum, even if the words it employed had to be carefully neutralized. The Christian pastoral prescribed as a fundamental duty the task of passing everything having to do with sex through the endless mill of speech. The forbidding of certain words, the decency of expressions, all the censorings of vocabulary, might well have been only secondary devices compared to that great subjugation: ways of rendering it morally acceptable and technically useful. (p. 21)

The results of such discourse are, of course, readily apparent in that endless stream of hysterical females in nineteenth-century literature, from Marianne Dashwood in *Sense and Sensibility* (1811) to Hedda Gabler (1890). I say females, not because males are free from the consequences of sexual repression and social engineering, but because in a patriarchal society they remain dominant within the discourse – essentially its beneficiaries rather than its victims. One has only to consider at the most superficial level the language of Freud to recognize this male-dominated sense of our sexual and social psychology. Women apparently, and in Freudian terms, mourn the absence of that which they envy: or – even in the face of the neurological evidence – as a girl becomes a woman, the locus of her sexual pleasure shifts from the clitoris to the vagina; she becomes what culture demands despite, not because of, the body. Sex, in other words, is allied closely to religion, and becomes an artifice in the configured narratives of our lives.

Why am I insisting on this particular story? I do so because I want to examine the way in which texts impose themselves on our bodies to the extent that we speak in terms of such artifacts as natural or unnatural, and bodies themselves become texts uneasily and disturbingly present in interpreted and coercive con-texts. Nowhere is this coercion more powerful than in the Bible, and the tradition which has depended so largely upon the canonical authority of the texts of scripture for its immense influence on us and our culture. Bodies, I suggest, must be recognized as violated in order to recover a sense of their essential vitality – a disturbing literary return to theological possibilities. For it is extraordinary how the freedom of art and literature can, so often, offend the accepted tradition to the extent that it reveals, most shockingly, the repressive, even escapist, hypothesis which underlies our reading of sacred scripture. In his study of the strategies of sexual politics over two thousand years, Thomas Laqueur remarks:

> I have found it impossible in all but isolated forays into literature, painting, or the occasional work of theology to imagine how such different visions of the body worked in specific contexts to shape passion, friendship, attraction, love. A colleague pointed out to me that he heard Mozart's *Cosi fan tutti* with new ears after reading my chapters about the Renaissance. I have felt a new poignancy in the tragicomedy of eighteenth-century disguise – the last act of *Nozze di Figaro,* for example – with its questioning of what it is in a person that one loves. Bodies do and do not seem to matter. I watch Shakespeare's comedies of sexual inversion with new queries, and I try to think my way back into a distant world where the attraction of deep friendship was reserved for one's like.
>
> Further than that I have not been able to go. I regard what I have written as somehow liberating, as breaking old shackles of necessity, as opening up worlds of vision, politics, and eros.[2]

Before one dangerously breaks the shackles, however, one needs to observe the functioning of the discourse of repression, seen in literature, quite literally in stories of enslavement and imprisonment.

For example, Franz Kafka's story *In the Penal Settlement* (1919)[3] explores the inscribing on the bodies of convicted prisoners the text demanded by their sentences. Kafka is arguably, and perversely, the most biblical of modern Jewish writers, along with Freud compelling a recognition of rupture in the tradition even while they long for continuity.

Heinz Politzer notes Kafka's translation in *In the Penal Settlement* of proverb into an image: "he who refuses to hear must feel", with its German word-play *hören, horchen, gehorchen,* and its ironic play upon the biblical text.[4] In the story the "Harrow", as the artifice which effects the inscription on human flesh, is presented as a machine which is to be observed in operation by a "reader" who is not involved in the processes of textuality, one known as "the explorer". The prisoner, it is made clear, does not know the nature of the sentence which has been passed on him. "There would be no point in telling him. He'll learn it corporally, on his person."[5] Indeed, the prisoner does not even know that a sentence has been passed on him – no chance of a defence can be offered. What one *is* can never be a matter of personal decision or negotiation. It is the nature of the officer's orthodoxy – as another version of Dostoevsky's Grand Inquisitor – that guilt is never to be doubted. The language which he uses to describe the Harrow is unnervingly biblical, in the sense that it concentrates on the mode of establishing the textuality of orthodoxy, and avoids the moral implications of the case itself.

The instructions which regulate the machinery of the Harrow are closely guarded by the officer, and have to be interpreted like a biblical text to the explorer, the point being made that "It's no calligraphy for school children. It needs to be studied closely. I'm quite sure that in the end you would understand it too. Of course the script can't be a simple one" (p. 178). There is a chilling moment of comparison here with Paul's point in I Corinthians 3: 3, when he reminds his readers that they are still not ready for the "solid food" of his text, but must be kept, like Kafka's explorer, in a childish, uninformed condition.

Finally, in Kafka's story, we are reminded that the letter both defines and kills – it makes the prisoner what he is, and also brings about his death. Decipherment, that is, "true" reading, takes place for the prisoner when the text is not read as text, but becomes himself fully, and that is also the moment of death (a moment clearly recognized by Roland Barthes when he observes in *Writing Degree Zero* (1953) that literature "shines with its maximum brilliance at the moment when it attempts to die"):

> Enlightenment comes to the most dull-witted. It begins around the eyes. From there it radiates. A moment that might tempt one to get under the Harrow with him. Nothing more happens after that, the man only begins to understand the inscription, he purses his mouth as if he were listening. You have seen how difficult it

> is to decipher the script with one's eyes; but our man deciphers it with his wounds .... By that time the Harrow has pierced him quite through and casts him into the grave .... (p. 180)

Finally, in the story, the Harrow ceases to function, its silent working "a delusion". The machine ceases to write a text, but merely jabs and wounds, the officer himself its victim in a confusion of blood. The writer its final and greatest victim, the maker of textuality is revealed as simply the purveyor of incomprehensible suffering. Kafka's story can reveal to us the violation which is taking place within the protected canonicity of the sacred text – violation being of the body, itself now textual, which suffers under the longed-for authority of textual truth and authority.

The language and themes of Toni Morrison's novel *Beloved* (1987) are closely linked with a later theme of the present study which is the necessary complication and inversion of traditional apocalypse in contemporary literature[6] (see Chapter 8). In this startling novel bodies are subjected to violence and "disfigurement", and the black victims of violence inflict violence on their own bodies as a means of violating that male, white "order" which can only respond as to something alien and mysterious. I refer to just two moments in this immensely complex and structured–deconstructed text.

Sethe is a black woman born into slavery in Kentucky in the mid-1880s. Near the beginning of the novel Paul D returns to her home and moves in:

> He rubbed his cheek on her back and learned that way her sorrow, the roots of it; its wide trunk and intricate branches. Raising his fingers to the hooks of her dress, he knew without seeing them or hearing any sigh that the tears were coming fast. And when the top of her dress was around her hips and he saw the sculpture her back has become, like the decorative work of an ironsmith too passionate for display, he could think but not say, "Aw, Lord, girl." And he would tolerate no peace until he had touched every ridge and leaf of it with his mouth, none of which Sethe could feel because her back skin had been dead for years.[7]

Later the metaphor is developed and Sethe's back is described as a chokecherry tree in bloom (though dead). The result of beatings, the comment is made: "What God have in mind, I wonder" (p. 79).

Sethe's fate is the same as the prisoners in Kafka's story. Her own body is her text, a violation which she can neither see nor feel, since its inscription renders her insensitive to it. Paul D, however, finds himself forced to "read", though not with his eyes – with the implication, as in all our merely visual "readings" of such bodily texts, of a morbid voyeurism – but with his mouth, that is by loving touch. To change slightly Kafka's proverb: "he who cannot see must feel". He kisses the unread, unreadable yet inescapable text which has been inflicted on Sethe's body. And it is Paul D's love which eventually alone can save Sethe from the insanity which follows her act of infanticide on her baby, "Beloved", her attempt to save her child from the violation of textual inscription which had been her fate in the "order" of a white man's world.

The second moment of violation involves Paul D himself, when as a slave he is unable to speak to Sethe's first husband because a bit has been placed in his mouth. Quite literally his body is rendered silent and without means of verbal communication. The grin which the bit forces is a hideous distortion of free "body language". What the narrative stresses is the deep need to *speak* of such suffering, and to verbalize it, as Sethe recognizes that "he wants to tell me . . . He wants me to ask him about what it was like for him – about how offended the tongue is, held down by the iron, how the need to spit is so deep you cry for it" (p. 71). The victims of such torture retain the "text" on the bodies in the persistent "wildness of the eye".

Morrison's novel explores the way in which bodies are inscribed because of race and gender, the isolating effect of such inscription, and the need to violate those very texts themselves in what Mark Ledbetter ambiguously, and rightly, calls "an act that repulses their enslavers and binds the once enslaved into a community of the damned and pained, but now free and prepared for body healing".[8] Tragically, the story is told and remembered, Sethe's word for it is "rememory", just as the story in religious history is re-enacted and a memorial liturgically celebrated in a *sacrifice* of thanksgiving. Yet, at the same time, the textuality of pain must itself be obliterated and a new start made, at once the same yet different. (Perhaps, as in the biblical story, the text must be redrawn, not simply revived.) And so, Morrison concludes *Beloved* with the repeated refrain, "It was not a story to pass on" (pp. 274–5). Yet still her last word is "Beloved".

Kafka and Morrison, from their different traditions – the mid-European Jew and the African-American – force our "textual gaze" from the written page to the inscribed body. And so I move now to some reflections on images in pictorial art as well as literature, in which the scriptural text is literally transcribed on to bodies, and, I suggest our configurations of the familiar stories are shaken so that the form of the human body as represented in our reading of the canonical literature is necessarily redrawn and the canon "deconstructed" into a mode which literature recognizes immediately as the tragic. Finally, and above all, the reshaping of the coherence of salvation history is seen to become not only the tragedy of men and women in pain, but the tragedy of God himself, and theology must either abandon its task, or else profoundly reconfigure itself with unwonted humility.

The story of doubting Thomas in John 20: 24–9 is familiar enough to most Western readers. Indeed, we probably hardly feel the need to return to the text itself so well-known is the episode, so that when we look at the startling painting attributed to Caravaggio now in the Neues Palais, Potsdam, we recognize immediately the reference and instinctively, so to speak, "read" the painting from the remembered text. Caravaggio (1573–1610) (some art historians question whether the picture is actually by Caravaggio; that argument is not pertinent to my discussion here), however, has apparently deliberately "misread" and even coarsened the text of the Gospel, which familiarly runs:

> Then he said to Thomas, "Reach your finger here; see my hands. Reach your hand here and put it into my side. Be unbelieving no longer, but believe." Thomas said, "My Lord and my God!" (v. 27)

Reading Caravaggio's painting from this pre-text, we recognize with horror that in it Thomas is actually feeling within Christ's wounded side with his extended forefinger and with exaggerated scepticism. His rude penetration of Christ's proffered side is a vulgarizing of the biblical narrative, a closer reading of its delicate shading. Two other figures, unmentioned in the Gospel, crouch closely over Thomas's shoulder as Christ's left hand actually guides his intrusive finger into the gaping flesh. Thus, that which canonically is a story of faith in the risen Christ, becomes in art a terrible moment of profound scepticism, even voyeurism, discovered within the religious text.

If Caravaggio complicates and humanizes the biblical configuration of the story of a truly doubting Thomas, raising again the question of the nature of Christ's risen body for theology and in human belief, Rembrandt's great portrayal of Bathsheba receiving her summons from King David reverberates with an even more intense sense of tragedy in his "mis-reading" of the text of II Samuel 11. I have already referred briefly to this great painting in Chapter 1 (see pp. 4–5), and to the way in which art has focused upon and developed the almost transparent scriptural figure of the woman in the story. Here is the biblical text:

> It happened, late one afternoon, when David arose from his couch and was walking upon the roof of the king's house, that he saw from the roof a woman bathing; and the woman was very beautiful. And David sent and enquired about the woman. And one said, "Is this not Bathsheba, the daughter of Eliam, the wife of Uriah the Hittite?" So David sent messengers and took her; and she came to him, and he lay with her. (vv. 2–4)

As with the Caravaggio, the picture, dating from 1654 and now in the Louvre, is "read", in the first instance, from the "pre-text" of the biblical narrative, and the immediate correspondences tend to blind us to the incongruencies between these two "texts". There is, in the background of the painting, merely the slightest hint of a rooftop, but no David is anywhere in sight. The strong focus on Bathsheba's [almost] naked body seemingly concentrates on the detail mentioned only after her intercourse with David, that she was engaged in purifying herself after her period. The servant at her feet is clearly drying her right foot with a cloth. Yet the purifying is, ambiguously, also her toilet, her beautifying for the love-making which is to come. Virtually naked, Bathsheba is nevertheless gloriously adorned with jewels – in her hair, around her neck, her arm, and with splendid earrings.

Such ambiguity is present in other ways to offer and disrupt the "narrative" of the painting – a narrative which confuses and alters the tragedy of the biblical narrative. For if King David is nowhere present in the painting, the viewer instead is drawn into the bewitchment which is the King's in the scriptural story. It is we who see Bathsheba as David saw her, naked at her toilet. Rembrandt, indeed, lovingly humanizes the woman by using as his model Hendrickje Stoffels who lived with the artist after the death of his wife Saskia. Her beauty is all the more arresting because it is not idealized, even including the lump beside her left breast. Her body is turned to present itself fully to our gaze, so much so that the awkward position of her legs, crossed yet twisted so as to turn the torso, offers her breasts openly to view. Yet such a flaunting of her sexuality – simply the genitals lightly and carelessly covered and therefore all the more exposed – is belied only by her tragic, averted gaze, which may be looking at the figure of the servant kneeling at her feet, yet is more clearly directed meditatively inward to herself. Again, the narrative is at once suggested and denied.

And if our gaze is drawn, like David's, to the splendid body, it is diverted from it at the same time to the more brilliant whiteness of the letter grasped by Bathsheba, a letter which is crumpled and has clearly already been read by her. Now the messengers from David who come to fetch her to him bear no letter in the biblical story. They come in person and take her to the King. Only later in the tragic series of events is a letter mentioned – the letter of verse 14 which David writes to Joab, instructing him to ensure that Uriah the Hittite, Bathsheba's husband, is killed in battle. Is *this* the letter which has somehow gone astray into the hands of Uriah's wife, and been read here by Bathsheba prompting her inward gaze: a tragic letter which implicates the woman deeply in the death of her husband; a letter grasped by her in her exposed, beautified, unclean nakedness? Rembrandt's great, static picture rearranges the biblical narrative, and involves the "reader" in a tragic subversion of narrative which leaves the magnificent body of Bathsheba at once both its cause and its victim. We now cannot be sure, drawn as we are to that terrible, sorrowing gaze, whether this is a moment *before* or *after* Bathsheba's intercourse with David. Again the real, fleshly body is tragically in question, and it is a body of painful ambiguity disrupting the story of scripture.[9]

From Caravaggio and Rembrandt I move to a third Old Testament example of the body in pain, this time from literature, in the retracing of a biblical "pre-text" in Margaret Atwood's dystopic novel *The Handmaid's Tale* (1985). One's immediate recognition of the biblical images embedded in this visionary Republic of Gilead is repeatedly, and tragically, undercut by their logical misrepresentation. The tragic/comic logic of the narrative is underwritten by Atwood's initial quotation from Jonathan Swift's *A Modest Proposal*, with its ironic, and entirely logical, solution to "vain, idle, visionary thoughts". The scriptural references at the heart of the novel's sterility are Genesis 30: 1–3 (quoted as a preface by Atwood), and Genesis 16: 1–3:

> Abram's wife Sarai had borne him no children. Now she had an Egyptian slave-girl whose name was Hagar, and she said to Abram, "You see that the Lord had not allowed me to bear a child. Take my slave-girl; perhaps I shall found a family through her." Abram agreed to what his wife said; so Sarai, Abram's wife, brought her slave-girl, Hagar the Egyptian, and gave her to her husband Abram as a wife [concubine].

Now Sarai's proposal was certainly, both legally and morally, perfectly in accordance with custom. In the event of a woman's childlessness, a birth by her husband from her personal maid was considered to be the wife's legitimate child.[10] Yet, even in the biblical text, there is a suggestion of impropriety in the future relationship between mistress and maid. But what Genesis merely and faintly hints at, Atwood's narrative makes violently explicit. Her narrator is called Offred (of-Fred), the equivalent of the biblical slave-girls Bilhah and Hagar. She describes her sexual union with her Commander harshly and bitterly:

> My red skirt is hitched up to my waist, though no higher. Below it the Commander is fucking. What he is fucking is the lower part of my body. I do not say making love, because this is not what he is doing. Copulating too would be inaccurate, because it would imply two people and only one is involved. Nor does rape cover it; nothing is going on here that I haven't signed up for. There wasn't a lot of choice but there was some, and this is what I chose.[11]

The body of the woman has here become the literally open text which the biblical narrative conceals. By Offred herself her body is objectivized and dissected into parts. Critical language becomes clinical, and morality is briefly acknowledged only in order to be abandoned. As she later puts it, "One detaches oneself. One describes" (p. 106). Offred's body as text is now exposed to that exploitative rape which the textuality of Genesis both hints at and forbids, the scriptural "pre-text" here developed and, literally, exposed by a damaging, painful literality. Offred herself makes the bitter observation, "Context is all" (p. 154).

The Bible itself is embedded literally as well as metaphorically in the heart of *The Handmaid's Tale*.[12] The character of Commander (the biblical Abram or Jacob), keeps a copy of the scriptures locked in his room:

> He inserts the key, opens the box, lifts out the Bible, an ordinary copy, with a black cover and gold-edged pages. The Bible is kept locked up, the way people once kept tea locked up, so the servants wouldn't steal it. It is an incendiary device: who knows what we'd make of it, if we ever got our hands on it? We can be read to from it, by him, but we cannot read. (p. 98)

The Bible, an incendiary device, is not to be read, its textuality thereby denied. As a sacred text, it is to be kept secure – once let out for reading, its status becomes highly questionable, free from the constraints of authoritative canonicity. As we have seen, in art and literature, its narratives which bind bodies in the theological current of history rapidly become distorted as the textuality of the body asserts itself, and the body's tragedy revisits the configurations and conformities of scriptural orthodoxy. The question begins to arise in the midst of pain: whose tragedy is it in the end, of man or of God – and can these two be separated?

It has been suggested that whatever pain achieves, it achieves it to some extent through its unsharability and its resistance to language.[13] Pain, unsharably, is that which cannot be denied and cannot be confirmed, cannot be "read", and its resistance to language is of its essence – its solitariness at the very edge (and centre) of textuality. It evokes the deafening, unbearable, unheard scream of Edvard Munch. In Munch's celebrated picture the scream is unheard – the two figures in the distance pay no attention, yet it is deafening so that the haunted, central character covers her (why do I think it is the figure of a woman?) ears, and the whole landscape seems as if distorted by the sound-waves. What August Strindberg called the "scream of dread" is why the terrible, theologically justified narratives of the Bible are shredded in the wordless and tragic images of art which ineluctably transpose the biblical text on to the bodies which it both presents and ignores: the body of Bathsheba, the body of the Handmaid, even the body of Christ, each isolated, broken and abandoned – sacrificed. I make no apology here for my movement back and forth between poetics and "visual poetics", breaking down, as Mieke Bal would put it, the opposition between word and image in an extended sense of textuality so that "reading" becomes a broader, even more humanly demanding experience in the face of the unavoidable images of the body in art, where pain and ecstasy cannot be intellectualized or spiritualized away.

As we have already seen in Chapter 3, modern "literary" readings of the biblical text may almost be said to begin with Erich Auebach's close reading of the Akedah, the "sacrifice" of Isaac in Genesis 22. This narrative, described by the Old Testament scholar Gerhard von Rad as "the most perfectly formed and polished of all the patriarchal stories", has almost from the beginning perplexed and exercised midrashists and interpreters from many traditions. Søren Kierkegaard in *Fear and Trembling* and in letters writes of different Abrahams, attempting to fill the gap between verses 3 and 4 of the Genesis story, between Abraham's setting out and "the third day". For Kafka, who brooded long on Kierkegaard's readings, the Dane "doesn't see the ordinary man ... and paints this monstrous Abraham in the clouds",[14] a murderer who hates his son. For Kafka, Abraham presents a problem – not without precedent in Midrash – of mishearing or misunderstanding, almost anticipating the midrash of another modern Jewish writer, Woody Allen whose comic rendering places both Abraham and God in question. Thus:

> And so he took Isaac to a certain place and prepared to sacrifice him but at the last minute the Lord stayed Abraham's hand and said, "How could thou doest such a thing?
>
> And Abraham said, "But thou said –"
>
> "Never mind what I said," the Lord spake. "Doth thou listen to every crazy idea that come thy way?" And Abraham grew ashamed. "Er – not really ... no."
>
> "I jokingly suggest thou sacrifice Isaac and thou immediately runs out to do it."
>
> And Abraham fell to his knees. "See, I never know when you're kidding."
>
> And Lord thundered, "No sense of humor. I can't believe it."
>
> "But doth this not prove I love thee, that I was willing to donate mine only son to thy whim?"

And the Lord said, "It proves that some men will follow any order no matter how asinine as long as it comes from a resonant, well-modulated voice."

And with that, the Lord bid Abraham get some rest and check with him tomorrow.[15]

Here, indeed, is a narrative which guards its secrets, yet has also prompted powerful canonical readings within the patriarchal stories.

Here I want to concentrate upon the readings of the Akedah offered through the medium of visual art by Rembrandt, who has given us at least three versions of the story. Each version diverges significantly from the biblical narrative. In a beautiful etching of 1645, a richly clad and turbaned Abraham holds earnest conversation with his son at the place of sacrifice. To the left of the picture is the fire, an iron pot standing on the coals, while a huge knife hangs at the patriarch's side. Isaac stands quietly by with a bundle of firewood, while his father points upwards. In response to Isaac's question, "Here are the fire and the wood, but where is the young beast for the sacrifice?", Abraham replies, "God will provide himself a young beast for a sacrifice, my son" (vv. 7–8). In Genesis these words are spoken on the journey and not at the place where the sacrifice is being prepared. The effect of this small deviation is to heighten the potentially tragic tension in the intimacy of this trusting, familial moment from which God himself is excluded.

Very different are the two versions (more familiar in the history of art) of the later moment of the sacrifice itself, stayed by angelic intervention. Rembrandt's great painting of 1635 in St Petersburg is separated by twenty years from the tortured etching of 1655 in Amsterdam. The earlier painting, in the European baroque style, portrays Abraham, an old and white-bearded man, violently holding Isaac down, his hand covering the face and exposing the lad's neck to the blow, while the angel physically intervenes – unlike the angel of the Genesis narrative – forcing Abraham to drop the dagger from his right hand. In the 1655 etching Abraham is again aged and white-bearded, but his face is now sunken, the eyes inwardly staring in tragic weariness. Once more his hand covers Isaac's face, but with the opposite effect for the boy is now kneeling in a bending posture, while his father covers his eyes protectively from the knife. In each version, and in different ways, Abraham is a tragic figure, aged, powerful, weary, tortured. In the late etching in particular, the angel seems almost to embrace him, covering him with his wings.

What is so disturbing about these Rembrandt pictures? Each alters the biblical text in small but significant ways. In the 1645 etching God is pointed to, yet is altogether absent from the deep human correspondence between father and son. In the other two pictures, Abraham is anything but the turbaned eastern potentate: the age, the white beard – one is almost reminded of the other "character" in the story, God himself, were it not for Abraham's tortured, fatherly misery. Yet the tragic, divided figure of these paintings seems closest to the potentially divided divinity of Genesis – the God who seems to change his mind.

God, as God in the biblical story, is, of course, entitled to be consistently inconsistent though even some later midrashists were exercised by this and suggest that God, being unable to change his mind, allows the sacrifice to take place, before restoring Isaac to life.[16] The potential, however, is there for a tragedy involving child sacrifice – and that potential emerges once the images of art begin to interpret the narrative of Genesis, that is, once the textuality of the verbal story is taken into the textuality of bodily representation. What is striking about the polished narrative of Genesis 22 is its lack of any insight into Abraham's inner self. That insight, it may be said, is reserved in the suggestiveness of literature and art, for the more complex "character" of God.

In Rembrandt's white-haired old man, therefore, are we seeing a "murderer", senility, tragedy, Abraham, or God? One thing is clear – the image is of a tortured face, a text expressive of a father who, for some reason, has become involved in the sacrifice of his own son. In the canonical narrative, only one figure between Abraham and God actually experiences that trauma to the actual limit. Rembrandt's painting and etchings, therefore, are once again exposing a textuality of the body which is masked by biblical literality; an uncomfortable (mis-)reading of a text which is seen as an unrealized pretext for tragedy and a problem for theology.

Rembrandt's conscious or unconscious insight is taken up in the new context of human conflict by the poet Wilfred Owen in his poem of the Great War, "The Parable of the Old Man and the Young". The "angel of the Lord" of Genesis 22: 11 is here "an angel . . . out of heaven", (no mention is made of the Lord) saying:

> Lay not thy hand upon the lad,
> Neither do anything to him. Behold,
> A ram caught in a thicket by its horns;
> Offer the Ram of Pride instead of him.

But the old man would not so, but slew his son,
And half the seed of Europe, one by one.
(lines 11–16)

The last line clearly refers back ironically to Genesis 22: 17–18, with its promise to the "seed" of Abraham. But who is the "old man" of Owen's poem? Abraham, after all, was obedient to the angel. The hint that the tragedy might, in the first instance, be God's, becomes apparent in the recontextualized presentations of art and poetry. In Derek Jarman's 1988 film of Benjamin Britten's *War Requiem* (1962), which intersperses Owen's war poetry with liturgical texts, Owen's poem becomes even more suggestive in the *public* sacrifice enacted before a "congregation" of grotesque capitalists and profiteers, by a clerical figure, bearded, triumphant and satanic – anything but the Abraham of Genesis 22. Britten scores the poem as a duet between a tenor and a baritone, their final line "And half the seed of Europe, one by one" repeated three times as a series of six interruptions to the chorus of boys' voices singing the "Offertorium" of the *Missa pro Defunctis*, suggestive of innocents led to the slaughter.

"Context is all", Offred asserts in Atwood's tale. In Owen's poem, and mightily intensified in Britten's *Requiem* and Jarman's film, the biblical story is contextualized in the experience both of war and the liturgy, and, as when Rembrandt meditates upon the image of the sacrifice in art, the text emerges by its own violation revealed in the tragic, divided, cruel figure of Abraham/God.

This tragedy of God's body in the texts of art is underlined in the suggestions made recently by Kenneth Dauber in an essay entitled "The Bible as Literature: Reading Like the Rabbis".[17] Dauber makes the point that the Jewish Bible resists the grand project of knowing Being. There is, Dauber suggests, no concept of Being in the Bible, since "what it renders is not the revelation of an existence but the establishment of a certain relation. Accordingly, the Bible is not a text to be interpreted" (p. 27). Furthermore, Dauber argues that the telling of the Abraham story in Genesis resists all *context* (p. 29). He continues:

> In the midst of a larger tale, it yet asserts itself as its own first principle. Such a telling, as we have said, cannot exemplify anything but itself. Its movement, what now becomes the Bible, does not unfold some prior state, but, coming from nowhere, merely develops. For lack of a better term, and in honor of its traditional

war with philosophy, we may call this kind of telling literature. Literature is pure relationship, is the discourse of relationality. (p. 29)

I am not concerned to argue here with Dauber's thesis on Rabbinic reading, but I do disagree with this purist understanding of literature. For the intertextuality existing between Genesis and the texts in art, music, film and poetry exposes contexts (by exposure to contexts) which forcibly acknowledge the "being" of body, body in pain, isolated, resistant to language by its tragedy of suffering. Do Rembrandt's inwardly gazing Bathsheba, or "Abraham" (in the 1655 etching) have the benefit of a pure discourse of relationality? Their texts are their bodies, whose "being" they cannot escape: texts to which all philosophical reflection must finally and humbly return in a preoccupation only too familiar to philosophy at least since Heidegger, with Nietzsche before him.

If, as Dauber suggests, the Bible is not a text to be interpreted, then its canonical status from sacred story to sacred text, and its authority thereby, may remain principles for our assurance.[18] But what then of these violated, deeply contextualized images of art which disturb and divert the flow of biblical narrative? Above all, I am perplexed by the tragedy of God's body, the old man who, unlike the fortunate Abraham, actually sacrificed his son in an apocalypse of his own death.[19] Nowhere is the effect which Foucault so clearly perceives, of the control of the body and its sexuality, more tragically felt than in the body of the enfleshed-God of Christianity. (Any cursory review of patristic theological debate will reveal the inextricable relationship between Christological and Trinitarian controversy. God the Father cannot be extricated from the ambivalences of God the Son, and, arguably, only the Christological discussions of the Cappadocian fathers made the Chalcedonian Trinitarian resolution possible.)

The Christian tradition's neurotic fear of recognizing the implications of its fundamental belief in divine *incarnation* (embodying) emerge time and again in the docetic tendencies of its Christology – discernible as early as Luke's Gospel or even "doubting" Thomas himself (!), in the neurotic fear of sexuality expressed by Augustine in, for example, Book XXII of the *City of God* which is concerned with the resurrection body, and the seemingly inevitable tendencies of art to remind "orthodoxy" of its failure to "celebrate" the body in both its beauty and in its violated tragedy. Paradoxically, the central event of suffering in God's own person is too easily affirmed and hysterically denied when it confronts us in the images of art. Thus the very angularity of the figures in John Everett Millais's painting *Christ in the House of His Parents* (1849), with its balding Joseph and the untidiness of the workshop, evoked a howl of rage from no less a personage than Charles Dickens, when it was exhibited at the Royal Academy. Surely the God made flesh cannot be tolerated in this "hideous, wry-necked, blubbering, red-headed boy, in a bed gown".[20] Dickens's sensitivity is an example of what Leo Steinberg has called the "modern oblivion", that is, the cover-up, "profound, willed and sophisticated",[21] of the text of Christ's body, the body which, above all, exposes *us* to the tragedy of the suffering and death of God. Dickens's outrage has been repeated in our own time by responses to both Nikos Kazantzakis's book (and less importantly, Martin Scorsese's recent film) *The Last Temptation* (1959), blacklisted by the Vatican, of which the opening chapters portray a dismally sordid, even tragic, "holy family". Perhaps our very refusal to acknowledge the countless violations of the human body in history, beginning with the massive cover-up of the salvation history of the biblical narrative, littered as it is with broken, beaten, raped and discarded victims, has actually rendered us incapable of acknowledging the worst bodily inscription of all.

The Christian horror of the body finds its greatest early articulation in Augustine, for whom semen itself is "shackled by the bond of death" such that every human being ever conceived through semen already is born contaminated with sin.[22] Only Christ, Augustine argued, is free from sin since he was conceived without semen. Yet it was the art of the Renaissance, according to Steinberg, which offered for contemplation what theology has tended to deny, that Christ being enfleshed was also sexed and circumcised, and suffered the painful textuality of bodily violation and death.

Renaissance images of the Virgin accompanied by the Christ child with his genitals exposed and even presented, are common enough. Their purpose is serious and theological as an affirmation of the doctrine of the incarnation. More radically, perhaps, I conclude the present chapter with a brief reference to a group of fifteenth-century Flemish images, a sub-type of what are sometimes called the Trinity, or Throne of Grace.[23] In a fragment of 1443, after Rogier van der Weyden (perhaps the major artist of mid-fifteenth-century Flanders), the powerful figure of God the Father supports the exhausted figure of the Christ who is naked but for a loin cloth, his wounded hands presented. Most significantly, the Father's left hand covers the Son's groin, indicating his death to be that of a full man. Sin (sexuality) and death are equally present in the inconography of this work, the divine body of the Second Person read here as a text in an embodiment fastidiously avoided by the Church's Christology. Not only does such art disturb the narrative of the Church's official discourse and doctrine, as Rembrandt and Caravaggio do of the canonical narrative of the Bible, but it goes further in its profound unsettling of the almost universal taboo which separates, bodily, father from son, ultimately a real problem for Trinitarian theology. As James Joyce expressed it in *Ulysses* (1922), Episode IX: "They are sundered by a bodily shame so steadfast that the criminal annals of the world, stained with all other incests and bestialities hardly records its breach."

Yet here, in the art of the early Northern Renaissance, we find this very bestiality gloriously acknowledged in the godhead, the summit of all those entextualizations in art and literature of bodies exposed, tragically violated, inscribed upon, triumphant. What the sacred text denies, the unavoidable text requires – that we penetrate the wounded side of Christ, that we acknowledge that contextualizing of pain so that, after Rembrandt's great meditations on Abraham and Isaac, we acknowledge also what is meant by the divine tragedy, the death of God, the ultimate, unspeakable text. Only then might we be freed for a new Christology, one which Thomas Altizer has begun to articulate in apocalyptic terms, and is the subject of a later chapter. He writes:

> A contemporary Gnosticism is a flight from that apocalypse, or a flight from an overwhelmingly interior actuality of death as death, and death as an ultimate or eternal death, a death whose very unspeakability is the unspeakability of death, an unspeakability which is the unspeakability of our interior depths, which now are speakable only as either the absence or the abyss of any truly interior domain or realm.[24]

The readings of the biblical text which we have been considering in art and literature precisely draw us back from such a flight into which we may, so easily, be led. They force us to *look*, and in looking we realize afresh that which cannot merely be named, for to do so is to make it speakable, and therefore bearable. To face the tragedy which has been the theme of these last two chapters is to recognize the unspeakable, the unbearable which will not tolerate easy configurations or solutions. It is to revive and bring back to life that which otherwise may become dead and useless.

Such images as I have considered in this chapter are perhaps necessary to enable us to begin to *un*-read the canonical, public discourse and text of scripture, drawing us closer and more humanely to that absolute paradox (a Christological observation) which alone can enable us to continue to act or speak.

Notes

1. Michel Foucault, *The History of Sexuality*, vol. I: *An Introduction*, trans. Robert Hurley (Harmondsworth, 1981) p. 7.
2. Thomas Laqueur, *Making Sex: Body and Gender from the Greeks to Freud* (Cambridge, Mass., and London, 1990) pp. 23–4.
3. *In the Penal Settlement (In der Strafkolonie)* in the translation of Willa and Edwin Muir. An alternative title is *In the Penal Colony*, e.g. in Heinz Politzer, *Franz Kafka: Parable and Paradox* (Ithaca, N.Y., 1966). See Valentine Cunningham *In the Reading Gaol* (Oxford, 1994) pp. 386–8, for an account of the "biblical nature" of Kafka's story.
4. See Politzer, ibid., pp. 98–102. I am indebted to William Doty for drawing my attention to this point.
5. Franz Kafka, *In the Penal Settlement* (1919), in *Metamorphosis and Other Stories*, trans. Willa and Edwin Muir (Harmondsworth, 1961) p. 174.
6. See, further, T. Mark Ledbetter, "An Apocalypse of Race and Gender: Body Violence and Forming Identity in Toni Morrison's *Beloved*", in David Jasper (ed.), *Postmodernism, Literature and the Future of Theology* (London and New York, 1993) pp. 78–90.
7. Toni Morrison, *Beloved* (London, 1988) pp. 17–18.
8. Ledbetter, "An Apocalypse", p. 81.
9. For a marvellous discussion of this painting, see Mieke Bal, *Reading "Rembrandt": Beyond the Word–Image Opposition* (Cambridge, 1991) pp. 224–30.
10. See Gerhard von Rad, *Genesis: A Commentary*, rev. edn, trans. John H. Marks (London, 1963) p. 191.
11. Margaret Atwood, *The Handmaid's Tale* (1985; London, 1987) pp. 104–5.
12. For much of this discussion I am indebted to Dorota Filipczak, "Is There No Balm in Gilead? Biblical Intertext in *The Handmaid's Tale*", *Literature and Theology*, vol. 7, no. 2 (1993) 171–85.
13. Elaine Scarry, *The Body in Pain: The Making and Unmaking of the World* (Oxford, 1985) pp. 4–5.
14. Kafka in a letter to Max Brod of 1918, quoted in Jill Robbins, *Prodigal Son/Elder Brother: Interpretation and Alterity in Augustine, Petrarch, Kafka,*

Levinas (Chicago, 1991) p. 91. Robbins sustains a fine discussion of Kierkegaard and Kafka on the Akedah, pp. 89–97.

15. Woody Allen, "The Sacrifice of Isaac", *Apropos: An Almanac of the Humour and Satire of the World* (Sofia), no. 7 (1991) 71.
16. I am indebted to my colleague Robert Carroll for this observation. Even in the Genesis narrative God himself never rescinds the original command, but it is only effected at one remove. Clearly there is unease in the story at this point.
17. *Semeia*, vol. 31 (1985) 27–48.
18. See James A. Sanders, *From Sacred Story to Sacred Text* (Philadelphia, 1987), esp. ch. 1: "Adaptable for Life: the Nature and Function of Canon".
19. See, further, Thomas J. J. Altizer, *Genesis and Apocalypse: A Theological Voyage Toward Authentic Christianity* (Louisville, 1990).
20. Charles Dickens, *Old Lamps for New Ones*, quoted in Humphrey House, *The Dickens World*, 2nd edn (1942; Oxford, 1960) p. 126.
21. Leo Steinberg, *The Sexuality of Christ in Renaissance Art and Modern Oblivion* (New York, 1983) p. 109.
22. Before Augustine, a similar argument was made by Didymus the Blind, *Contra Manicheos* 8. See Elaine Pagels, *Adam, Eve and the Serpent* (London, 1988) p. 109.
23. See, Steinberg, *Sexuality of Christ*, pp. 106–8.
24. Altizer, *Genesis and Apocalypse*, p. 182.

5

The Bible and the Politics of Feminism

Already in the short space of this book readings of biblical texts have been invaded by a number of disciplines. How far may one entertain the claims of such a variety of discourses? To introduce yet another, therefore, the voice of feminist criticism, may seem foolhardy, particularly from one whose appreciation of feminism must always be borrowed: for as Toril Moi has somewhat tartly remarked: "with a few exceptions, the actual criticism produced by so-called male feminist critics is not overwhelmingly convincing".[1]

Nevertheless, feminist criticism has been a major voice in biblical studies in recent years, and with good reason. Indeed, there are a number of reasons. For just as the last chapter considered the body and sexuality in the pages and tradition of a scriptural canon which always seems to have assumed their erasure, so the concentration of feminist literary criticism on the Victorian era has articulated the repressed energies of female sexuality – and the disastrous consequences of its repression – in a period identified with prudery and, at best, perhaps, woman as the "angel in the house".[2] Foucault's *History of Sexuality*, among other works, has encouraged readings in Victorian literature in terms of its erotic energy – and the time is now with us when the Bible, swathed in its canonical correctness and orthodoxy as it is, must be similarly read – and exposed.

For in the dis-ease of theology, the Bible, like Victorian literature, is both obsessed with the body, yet repeatedly smothers it in a rhetoric which keeps it at arm's length from the reader even as it is being discussed. Paul, of course, is a principal culprit here, offering as he does to the Christian Church the central image of the body while saddling the tradition with a persistent and deathly neurosis regarding all bodily functions. He traps, it might be said, the body in discourse.

The liberation of the body, and particularly the female body, from the entrapment of language and discourse has been a proper preoccupation of much feminist writing. Entrapment may be a vicious form of control – but what will be the consequences of release from such slavery? The Victorian woman was the object of a rich, allusive language linking her body to her role as wife, mother, object of desire, and so on, yet she herself was denied access to that very same language. She was, effectively, silenced.[3] The result is the claustrophobic "buried life" of Lucy Snowe in Charlotte Brontë's *Villette*, the painful, depersonalizing lessons of Rachel Curtis in Charlotte Yonge's *The Clever Woman of the Family*, and the incarceration of the "madwoman" in *Jane Eyre*, Mary Elizabeth Braddon's *Lady Audley's Secret* and countless other Victorian novels. The same is true in the tradition of canonical reading of the Bible – we have seen how art and literature grant to Bathsheba a character and a tragic voice. Long before contemporary critics took up her cause, Rembrandt recognized the tragedy of the nameless concubine in Judges 19. More recently, as we shall see, a voice has been granted to Mary Magdalene in literature – the mysterious, wild girl of the New Testament.

The importance of feminist perspectives on biblical criticism is, in the end, political: the granting of a voice to that which within the text has been silenced. When Elizabeth Cady Stanton produced *The Woman's Bible* in 1895 and 1898, she conceived of it as a political act. She begins her Introduction thus:

> The canon and civil law; church and state; priests and legislators; all political parties and religious denominations have alike taught that woman was made after man, of man, and for man, an inferior being, subject to man. Creeds, codes, Scriptures and statutes, are all based on this idea. The fashions, forms, ceremonies and customs of society, church ordinances and discipline all grow out of this idea . . .
>
> The Bible teaches that woman brought sin and death into the world, that she precipitates the fall of the race, that she was arraigned before the judgement seat of Heaven, tried, condemned and sentenced.[4]

The Bible teaches . . . But Elizabeth Cady Stanton, like others who have followed her in contemporary criticism, reads *through* the configurations of the canonical narratives and reveals the human stupidity and heroism, the tragedy and comedy of life lived beneath their configured surface. Her dry assessment of Samson is worthy of Joseph Heller's King David: "It is a pity", she suggests, "that the angel who impressed on his parents the importance of considering everything that pertained to the physical development of the child, had not made some suggestions to them as to the formation of his moral character."[5] God in His wisdom . . . And, as her fellow writer the Reverend Phebe A. Hanaford points out, in the Book of Judges, whatever its *theological* place in the history of Israel, the women (where they are not sacrificed, raped or murdered without name or status) seem every bit as resourceful and persistent as the men. Delilah may be synonymous with woman tempting men to sin, but Samson was an ass, an overgrown schoolboy, and deserved all he got. The hero he may be, and "judge", but, as Stanton puts it, "one hesitates to decide which is most surprising – Samson's weakness or Delilah's wickedness".

The Woman's Bible with not a little wit and literary energy, proposes that the Bible is given to us as anything but "neutral". It is, rather, read as a political tool to be used against women and their legitimate demands, bearing the stamp of men who never saw or talked with God.[6] This *use* of the Bible needs to be revised through a feminist reading of the text which cuts through the translations and interpretations of men, deconstructing those criteria formulated by the theological demand for the "canon within the canon"[7] which steadies our "religious" appropriation of scripture within the tradition, a demand underwritten by historical-critical understanding of the canon. Elizabeth Cady Stanton stands alongside the artists and novelists with whom this book has already been concerned, shading its sense of the *human* tragedy of the biblical pages into a political, and in her day, deeply controversial debate which continues to our own time.

More generally feminism, and particularly the French feminism of the 1970s and 1980s which especially interests me, is inescapably political. Modern French women thinkers after Simone de Beauvoir and her ground-breaking work in *Le Deuxième Sexe* (1949), like Michèle le Doeuff, Arlet Farge and Annie Leclerc, have been deeply concerned to rewrite women back into the *history* of their culture and society. Their position never neutral, these thinkers seek to establish feminist or female space from which to speak and in doing so, among other things, have like Cady Stanton politicized existing critical methods in literary and other disciplines.

Allow me to offer the example of one particularly acute domestic issue in my own experience at the moment which is sharply problematized by this political and pluralistic quality of feminist debate. Recently the Church of England, of which I am a priest, has decided to break with tradition and ordain women to the priesthood. The immense and acrimonious divisions which have followed upon this decision have revealed starkly the muddled critical thinking which underlies much if not most of our so-called theological debates, but one point in particular troubles me. Inescapably, opponents of the decision tend to isolate the language and systematics of their position from the arena of debate which must at least consider the wide spectrum of feminist argument: in all other areas debate is permissible, but not here. Such absolutist claims separate, for me at least, theological claims from the arena within which must be argued out – reasoned out, if you will – all matters of judgement, value, aesthetics, morals, and finally even truth itself. One recognizes that one must be politically feisty, therefore, in order to keep theology – as I certainly wish to do – in court.

The second reason for putting myself in this present position as a "feminist" critic is that the political, and therefore argumentative, aspect of feminist debate, eschewing all virtuous neutrality, places it squarely within the business which must be central for all of us who call ourselves critics and not least critics of the Bible – that is the reasoned discussion of different possibilities. Our responsibility, indeed, is to abandon closed ways of thinking (with all their dangerous tendencies to authoritarian, totalitarian attitudes) which, as the feminist philosopher Michèle le Doeuff puts it, "cannot become diversified through encounters with different levels or fields of experience or with contingent facts".[8]

So what, then, of that particular field of criticism which concerns itself with the literature and canon of the Bible? Well, first, like all criticism, it must be a risky business, always looking around corners and taking chances, prepared even to make a fool of itself and working if need be by trial and error. That certainly was not my sense of the prim historical critical methods of biblical criticism which I was taught at Oxford, heavily impregnated as they were by nineteenth-century critical and philosophical assumptions and presuppositions. Such methods bore few marks of the *challenge* set, for example, by Stephen Moore in his recent books *Literary Criticism and the Gospels* (1989) and *Mark and Luke in Poststructuralist Perspectives* (1992) in whose image of the Parable of the Prodigal Son we, as critics, return home to present our harlots of criticism to the Father, they perhaps becoming in the process respectable, though, one hopes, not yet too domesticated. One wonders why the young Rembrandt in his early portrait of himself as the Prodigal living riotously portrays his own wife Saskia as the "harlot" on his knee, while X-ray photography has revealed an originally nude female in the background later painted over. Might the Prodigal not, in another version of the story, have presented his own legitimate *wife* to his father? It gives one, at least, pause for thought.

It was the Dutch critic Mieke Bal in her persistent "readings" of Rembrandt who suggested that "he may very well be considered Holland's most interesting biblical scholar".[9] Reading Bal's remarkable writings on biblical literature was, for me, a release from that systematic programme with which I had barely been aware I had been complicit, the profound Hegelianism of British biblical studies; doubly shocking when one reads again Hegel's anti-Semitic remarks and his characterization of women as "plant-like" – that is, complacent, cow-like and content. Bal is certainly none of these in her forays into feminist biblical hermeneutics and her sense of scripture's "inherent power to underscore power".[10]

The strength of Mieke Bal's reading of the Bible lies in her bold assertion of the role of critical theory in a crucial attentive dialogue with the text. No longer a mere servant in the business of excavating the truth hidden within the pages, critical theory, she asserts, cannot be meaningfully "applied" to the Bible any more than to any other body of texts. Theories are bodies of language of the same order as the text, with whom their relationship must therefore be dialogical. As two equals in conversation and encounter, critical theory (a rigorous and highly disciplined exercise) and text together will promote, and should expect, both relationship and confrontation in a healthy process of change, its success measured in terms of relevance and of limits. This very dialogue will tend towards a transgression not only of disciplinary boundaries, but also to a rewriting and reconfiguration of the history which our religious *readings* of the text – selected by lectionary and theology – tend to impose upon it. Inevitably, Bal would argue, such readings rapidly assume a patriarchal tone leading to the exclusion of women. Her critical dialogue will contribute to a mending of what Arlette Farge calls "the omissions of history". Herein, Farge continues,

> the marginalized, the deviant, the insane, the imprisoned and the sick were becoming historical subjects; all the figures "hidden from history" were being rehabilitated . . . , and women naturally numbered amongst them.[11]

What we are moving towards here is a reconstruction of the notion of "religious reading" of the Bible,[12] a reading not shackled to the games of power politics, but committed to open friendship in community, not to restriction but to celebration and acceptance, a rich, festive encounter which acknowledges the range of human experience from comedy to tragedy in a carnival of excess. Religious reading takes us out of ourselves in a loving acceptance of the other, so that, like the Prodigal Son at the moment of his enlightenment, we may "come to ourselves" (Luke 15: 17) anew and in a fresh spirit. To read religiously is a dialogical act and it is to recover the deeply serious/playful act of true worship, recognizing not the canon within the canon, but the world embraced and affirmed in the mystery of texts which survive in spite of all configurations.

But we need to get to grips with some solid texts lest we are accused of womanish meanderings. In Henry James's novel *Portrait of a Lady* (1881) – which the misogynist Jean-Paul Sartre could never finish (presumably offended by the portrayal of such a delightful and gifted woman as Isabel Archer[13]) – the dilettante Gilbert Osmond expresses his opinion of the "lady", Isabel Archer, whom he is about to marry:

> "I like her very much. She's all you described her, and into the bargain capable, I feel, of great devotion. She has only one fault."
> "What's that?"
> "Too many ideas."
> "I warned she was very clever."
> "Fortunately they're very bad ones," said Osmond.
> "Why is that fortunate?"
> "*Dame*, if they must be sacrificed!"[14]

Women in the Bible, of course, have always been handy when a sacrifice is required. Jephthah's daughter is a prime example (Isaac, of course, gets off scot free), or, more vindictively and less sacrifically – though no less finally – Samson's miserable wife at the hands of the Philistines.

Theories of sacrifice, of course, abound, and I select just one, not only because it has been influential, but because, coming from a sociologist it is calculated to annoy the average biblical critic. Emile Durkheim in *The Elementary Forms of Religious Life* (1912) views sacrifice as one of religion's important functions in unifying society. According to Durkheim, sacrifice is the metaphorical extension of a moral reality, namely, the interdependence of individual and society. Through the sacrifice of a victim, worshippers in a community both commune with their god and at the same time make an offering to the god. Sacrifice is both communion and oblation.[15] This, it seems to me, may be fine for society, but it doesn't do a great deal for the individual woman who is sacrificed. Jephthah's daughter could no doubt feel comforted that the daughters of Israel went year by year for four days to commemorate her, to recount her fate as an acknowledgement of what history requires, a memorialization of the patriarchal history. The girl's death, after all, enables the history of the father and the institutions of the state to progress.

What I am suggesting here, following Mieke Bal's lead, is that there is in the biblical text a "countercoherence" – we *read* the history of the Book of Judges as a procession of patriarchal wars (or patriarchal deviations from the way), while in the "orality" of the text the daughters of Israel and their tragedies recount the price that such a history requires. The point is that the discourses of theology, religious history or even sociology will propose theories which enable us to construct and configure our history within society, while within the great texts of the Bible – read so carefully and protectively – lurk the voices and memorials of those dehistoricized individuals who have been sacrificed "for the greater good".

Where the feminist criticism of recent decades becomes more awkward and threatening, indeed more articulate, in *its* readings of scriptures, is in its greater awareness of the issue of institutions. In France in particular and in the first instance, since de Beauvoir, it has become, in a word, more *political*. Biblical critics like Elisabeth Schüssler Fiorenza and Phyllis Trible have followed suit. Making good the omissions of history and writing women into history is a marked development from Simone de Beauvoir's pioneering work *Le Deuxième Sexe*. Beauvoir there restricts herself to the analysis of relations between individuals rather than the operation of socio-legislative (and, we may add, religious) structures. In other words, her discussion omits an analysis of institutions and therefore also a concept of exploitation.[16]

The Bible has always been a book which has promoted and

sustained institutions, while paradoxically at the same time posing a threat to those very same structures. Herein is what Mieke Bal calls its "countercoherence" which is another expression of the tension described in Chapter 3 between the canon and the disturbing presence of the "classics" of literature within it. The Christian Church, certainly, has always been acutely aware of the dangers of allowing people – anyone – actually to *read* the Bible. Even as ardent a supporter of the vernacular in scripture and the liturgy as Archbishop Thomas Cranmer in the English Protestant tradition had his doubts. For if in his 1540 Preface to the *Great Bible,* Cranmer was adamant that the Bible should be translated in each age so that people should "read and understand", his assent to the use of English in Church worship faltered before "certain mysteries, whereof I doubt" its appropriateness. As one modern commentator has well expressed it, "Beautiful veils before the holy of holies may inspire a sense of transcendent mystery, but they may also ensure that God 'the devouring fire' never comes anywhere near devouring *us.*"[17] Lectionaries tend to insure that our "reading" of the Bible is carefully controlled, cutting out awkward, unwanted elements. And generally the Church and the Synagogue have preferred to read the Bible *to* us, from big unwieldy volumes on lecterns which you could not carry out of the building even if you wanted to. Sometimes they are even chained down, they are so holy: or dangerous. We have already seen in Chapter 4 how in Margaret Atwood's novel *The Handmaid's Tale,* the Bible is kept locked away, read *to* the handmaids by their Commander. It is, after all, "an incendiary device". And once the text is thus removed from immediate scrutiny, who knows – from its very inception as a sacred book – what sleight of hand is being exercised by those in authority? In Atwood's novel, the handmaids, like members of a "religious order", have the Beatitudes read to them during lunch. The reading is alien to them in a two-fold manner, for it is not by a reader who is present but from a disc, and the voice is not a woman's but a man's. Here the text is inaccessible to any response or criticism; there is no sense of dialogue in this "religious" reading:

> Blessed be this, blessed be that. They played it from a disc, the voice was a man's. *Blessed be the poor in spirit, for theirs is the kingdom of heaven. Blessed are the merciful. Blessed are the meek. Blessed are the silent.* I knew they made that up, I knew it was wrong, and they left things out, but there was no way of checking.[18]

In the workings of the tradition, in the devices of scholarship, there rarely is.

Most of us, at points like this, quickly find defensive reasons to assert that "it's not like that for us". To which I reply, but of course it is. All we who have been taught to read, read in a particular way under the aegis of particular rules and theories (inescapably political) and as a result we see certain things and omit others. Inevitably we all read selectively as a protection, and that is not necessarily an altogether bad thing, as long as we are aware that the text, and especially *these* texts – for reasons I shall suggest in a moment – are liable, in that time-honoured word, to deconstruct our structures and institutions of reading revealing thereby those individuals who are hidden in and from history.

Since I am already deep in the game of critical pluralism, allow me now a little experiment in reading the "texts" of two further paintings to add to the glossolalia already in play. Let us see if two non-verbal images will contribute to the story we are trying to tell in this chapter. *The Kiss*, painted 1907–8, is perhaps one of the Austrian artist Gustav Klimt's best known pictures. It is usually read as an image of beautiful sexual fusion, a blissful moment of fulfilment between a loving couple drenched in gold and stars. But look closer before the painting's sensuality blunts your vision. For the woman's hand around the man's neck is clenched and taut. His hand beneath her bent head, does it support her or clamp her face to his? Her eyes are closed, but is this the oblivion of surrender, or the darkness of resistance? The painting quickly becomes a troubling mixture of fusion and alienation – a duck-rabbit of a picture which unpicks itself in every detail. We can easily convince ourselves that what we see is perfect love, and to see that is to *refuse* to see that the picture is what it is (a scene of rape) by being, at times, what it is not: fusion/alienation.

Now a very different painting, though again focusing upon a man and a woman. Rembrandt's early canvas of Mary Magdalene and the risen Jesus in the garden, from John 20, now in the Royal Collection is, so it is often said, charming, delightful and, to me at least, deeply troubling. It portrays the instant before Mary's recognition of Jesus, when she is surprised by one whom she takes to be the gardener. Jesus is a swashbuckling figure in a broad-brimmed hat, with spade in hand and a dagger in his belt. Mary is kneeling on the steps which lead up to a cavernous tomb in which sit two angels. Two other, presumably male, figures, seemingly richly clad, are walking away from the scene with apparent total unconcern, in the bottom left-hand corner of the picture. These two figures – are they disciples? – are not present at this moment in the Johannine narrative. Why does Rembrandt add them? Is it to expose even more Mary's solitude, unprotected in her fearfulness even by those who might be expected to protect her? For Mary's face wears an expression of fear, her body and the gesture of her hands are towards the "empty" tomb. But her face is turned, looking over her shoulder at the figure of Jesus behind her, half her face (that towards the tomb) being in shadow, the other half (that towards Jesus) illuminated, revealing her startled, worried, fearful gaze. She does not, of course, realize at this moment who the person is. She assumes that he is a strange, intrusive man, possibly the gardener, intruding upon her grief. The two angelic figures in the tomb seem blithely unconcerned. And as far as Mary herself is concerned, as in Klimt's picture of *The Kiss*, what we see is an experience of *angst* – actually not a charming painting at all, but a rather nasty image of a lone woman surprised by a man, armed with a knife, and, for all she knows, up to no good. We warn our daughters about just such men, especially when you meet them alone in the park. And if Klimt portrays a moment of close physical embrace, Rembrandt has taken that moment in the story when Jesus refuses Mary that physical contact which would reassure her – "noli me tangere". Of course, it is all in a good cause, any Christian worth his (or her) salt will tell you that, but it is a bit hard on Mary. No, this Easter day picture bothers me by its being, at times, what it is not.

I was actually reminded of this painting by Rembrandt, and came to read its version of the gospel narrative more closely, when I read the account of the same incident in Michèle Roberts's novel *The Wild Girl* (1984), which is a "fifth gospel" – an account of Jesus's teaching and his relationship with Mary, as told by Mary herself. The woman, as in Rembrandt's picture in a way, is given a voice. Just as in the Bathsheba story, the biblical non-person becomes a person, and disturbs the narrative of the canonical story. Though modern biblical scholarship studiously distinguishes separate figures in the gospel accounts of Mary – Mary of Bethany, the sister of Martha and Lazarus, the sinful woman who anoints Christ – Roberts follows the tradition of medieval and later art, legends and literature (and, not insignificantly, the Nag Hammadi texts) and portrays a composite figure who is articulate, real and powerful. As Roberts herself expresses it, she both dissects and recreates a myth, re-orientates by disorientation.[19]

Here there are not angels (dramatically excluded by Rembrandt as well), but simply an encounter between two people, and a dialogue which considerably expands the words spoken in the biblical narrative:

> – Don't touch me, he said, and then smiled at me, to show that he did not mean his words to hurt.
> – Why can't I touch you? I blurted out, not understanding anything.
> – I'm here with you now, he said: and I shall be with you always. I shall never leave you. But I am not in the body as I was before. We cannot love each other now as we did before. You know this already in your heart.
>
> I did not want to hear him say it. My joy at seeing him was mixed with sharp pain, as had so often been the case in the weeks before his death, when I embraced him and tasted the sweetness of his mouth and felt his arms around me and at the same time feared for him, feared for his safety, for the moment when the soldiers would come and take him away. I looked at his face, which was always beautiful to me and prayed for the courage to accept the truth he offered me. A little came, so that when I spoke my voice was steady.[20]

In *The Wild Girl,* as elsewhere in literature, as far back as early gnostic "gospels", Jesus and Mary are portrayed, daringly, as lovers. Here there is no embarrassment about the body. And so the smooth, unruffled narrative of John 20: 11–18 is disturbed by Mary's ambiguous feelings: her sense of pain and hurt at this merely "spiritual" presence; not so much the joy but the *courage* needed to accept the truth of the resurrected Lord.

In Rembrandt's painting and Roberts's novel we see the beautiful configuration of the sepulchre meeting between Jesus and Mary in the text of the Fourth Gospel disturbed and complicated by Mary's all-too-human responses. We see now fear, confusion, anger and resentment. We see her not obediently joyful at the gospel message, but rather her pain born of the denial of the womanly part of herself. In Roberts's version, we see Mary learning to control her own feelings with great effort. The joy of Easter is not bought cheaply.

Art, like all critical and "religious" reading as I here understand it, quickly sets up a dialogics which, if we are prepared to reckon with it, problematizes the institutions and the theology which govern our "official" taught reading, our particular historicizing of the canonical texts. Behind Rembrandt and Michèle Roberts lurk the politics of feminism. I agree profoundly with Terry Eagleton (though I disagree equally as profoundly with his particular arguments and reasoning) that literary theory – indeed, more broadly, critical theory – is unavoidably political.[21] The "political" consequences (in a way proposed by Elizabeth Cady Stanton) are precisely why most biblical critics, in my experience, remain almost the last people to assimilate critical theory into their procedures. Too quickly it spoils those methodologies which they "apply" to the Bible in order to preserve its inherited, canonical authority. Too quickly it triggers those countercoherences in the text which reveal the oppressions and exclusions at work in their closed ways of thinking. You see, I am not here resolving difficulties, I am *making* difficulties, and not apologizing for it, either!

Take, for instance, the story of Adam and Eve in Genesis 1–3. To say that it bristles with "literary" problems is an understatement. But what have religious people, in various times and places, made of those problems? Quite simply, they have spirited them away, or, more bluntly, *used* them, by blatantly reading the creation story quite differently, even antithetically, according to the needs and demands of circumstances – in the Christian Church as it changed from a dissident Jewish sect to a popular movement persecuted by the Roman government, to an institution in Roman society finally embraced by the Emperor himself.[22] This story is always flattened out according to circumstantial demand, and ultimately to promote, at the hands of St Augustine, extreme sexual neurosis, largely because he could not stand by his own woman or escape from his mother. The consequences for the Christian tradition can hardly be overestimated. And it takes a poet, John Milton, struggling in *Paradise Lost* with an intractable theological problem which he had already tried to tackle in the prose work *De Doctrina Christiana*,[23] but a poet for all that, to show us, in spite of himself, the obvious in Eve (Christian theology wraps the same problem up very delicately in the idea of a mother who remains a virgin – an odd idea which it is seemingly prepared to defend to the hilt), that the only way she could have resisted the serpent and remained "innocent" would be if she already had the canniness and insight of the fallen and "experienced". As it is, she is credulous, but credulity is part of her innocence. The outcome is a foregone conclusion. She cannot do other than fall. Read straight, the story is so obvious it is hardly worth the telling.[24]

Countercoherence again. Let the Bible loose and it becomes an incendiary device, making difficulties, but recalling us at the same time to political awareness, that is, a situation that must be debated in the knowledge that our readings both tend to closure and at the same time to encounters with different levels of experience. Feminist criticism has been, for me at least, a particularly powerful element in so far it has forced me into rigorous, systematic application through a concern for very real problems – that women all too often are written out, dehistoricized, flattened, in the march of biblical reception. The problem of sexual difference is central to feminist politics or theory, since the reason why women as a social group and as individuals are oppressed is precisely and simply that they differ from men.[25] And it is this difference which is so painfully explored, not in the gospel narrative, but in the artistic and literary examinations of Mary's experience in the garden, beside the empty tomb.

The strong assertion of difference is a political act. It is also a critical one in the crucial business of learning, and always relearning, to read, and specifically to read these texts.

Why these texts? It is because they are, in the end and in spite of all, still escapably *theological*. After the sacrifice of Jephthah's daughter, the daughters of Israel maintain her memory, so that she is remembered as what she was never allowed to be except in her non-being, that is, part of the progressive history of Israel. She is remembered as she was, in submissive non-being, the price of history, written out, de-historicized. Could this fragile girl actually be a clue to the nature of theological writing?

For if a text is that in which the meaning instantiates the world meant, and then, by pursuing the possibility of treating human existence (that which Heidegger called *Dasein*), shows the meaning of coming to be and passing away – in such a framework, theological text, as the writing of God, is what no actual text is: a theological text is the nontext of any "actual" text.[26] Countercoherence: even in Jahweh himself. In one fragile girl – as in Mary in the garden – we read, miraculously, a text which is what it is by being, at times, what it is not: the other of any text. Mary Magdalene is frightened by the stranger – who would not be? She is denied the hug which she might legitimately expect from one whom she loved so dearly and above all else. It was all wrong, it did not fit, it does not fit. That is the point which Rembrandt forces us to *see*, in his painting. We see it unavoidably, without elision or editorial omission. Just as Elizabeth Cady Stanton forces us to see the plain human dramas of Samson and David – seen in all their sinfulness, passion and tragedy – so we are forced to reckon with those whom history has written out of the story, recognizing interpretation as a political act with consequences for the "other", against the grain of belief and its permitted negotiations.

Notes

1. Toril Moi, "Feminist Literary Criticism", in Ann Jefferson and David Robey (eds), *Modern Literary Theory: A Comparative Introduction*, 2nd edn (London, 1986) p. 208.
2. See Helena Michie, *The Flesh Made Word: Female Figures and Women's Bodies* (Oxford, 1987): and, now classically, Sandra M. Gilbert and Susan Gubar, *The Madwoman in the Attic: The Woman Writer and the Nineteenth-Century Literary Imagination* (New Haven and London, 1984).
3. On women's inability to use bodily language, see Elaine Showalter, *A Literature of Their Own: British Women Novelists from Brontë to Lessing* (Princeton, 1977) pp. 26–7.
4. Elizabeth Cady Stanton, *The Woman's Bible*, Parts I and II (1898; Seattle, 1974) p. 7.
5. Ibid., Part II, p. 33.
6. See, further, Elisabeth Schüssler Fiorenza, *In Memory of Her: A Feminist Theological Reconstruction of Christian Origins* (London, 1983) pp. 7–14.
7. Ibid., p. 14.
8. Michèle le Doeuf, *Hipparchia's Choice: An Essay Concerning Women, Philosophy, Etc.*, trans. Trista Selous (Oxford and Cambridge, Mass., 1991) p. 194.
9. Mieke Bal, "Dealing / with / Women: Daughters in the Book of Judges", in Regina Schwartz (ed.), *The Book and the Text: The Bible and Literary Theory* (Oxford, 1990) p. 34.
10. Mieke Bal, *Death and Dissymetry: The Politics of Coherence in the Book of Judges* (Chicago, 1988) p. 38.
11. Arlette Farge, "Women's History: an Overview", in Toril Moi (ed.), *French Feminist Thought: A Reader* (Oxford, 1987) p. 136.

12. See, further, Robert Detweiler, *Breaking the Fall: Religious Readings of Contemporary Fiction* (London, 1989) pp. 30–66.
13. See le Doeuf, *Hipparchia's Choice*, pp. 192–3.
14. Henry James, *The Portrait of a Lady* (1881; Harmondsworth, 1966) p. 286.
15. See James G. Williams, *The Bible, Violence and the Sacred: Liberation from the Myth of Sanctioned Violence* (San Francisco, 1991) pp. 14–16.
16. See le Doeuf, *Hipparchia's Choice*, pp. 130–1.
17. David L. Frost, "Liturgical Language: Cranmer to Series 3", in R. C. D. Jasper (ed.), *The Eucharist Today: Studies on Series 3* (London, 1974) pp. 147–8.
18. Margaret Atwood, *The Handmaid's Tale* (London, 1987) pp. 99–100.
19. Michèle Roberts, *The Wild Girl* (1984; London, 1991) Author's Note.
20. Ibid., pp. 104–5.
21. Terry Eagleton, *Literary Theory: An Introduction* (London, 1983) "Conclusion: Political Criticism", pp. 194–217.
22. See Elaine Pagels, *Adam, Eve and the Serpent* (London, 1988) p. xxi.
23. Milton's *De Doctrina Christiana* was not printed until 1825. It makes explicit his theological unorthodoxy in its Arianism and doctrine of *creatio ex Deo*. See, specifically, Dennis Richard Danielson, *Milton's Good God: A Study in Literary Theodicy* (Cambridge, 1982) pp. 43ff.
24. Compare with this the pragmatic insight of Heller's King David into the business of killing Goliath. See above, Chapter 3. The obvious is often easiest to miss.
25. See Moi, *French Feminist Thought*, pp. 4–7.
26. See Robert P. Scharlemann, "Theological Text", *Semeia*, vol. 40 (1987) 5–19.

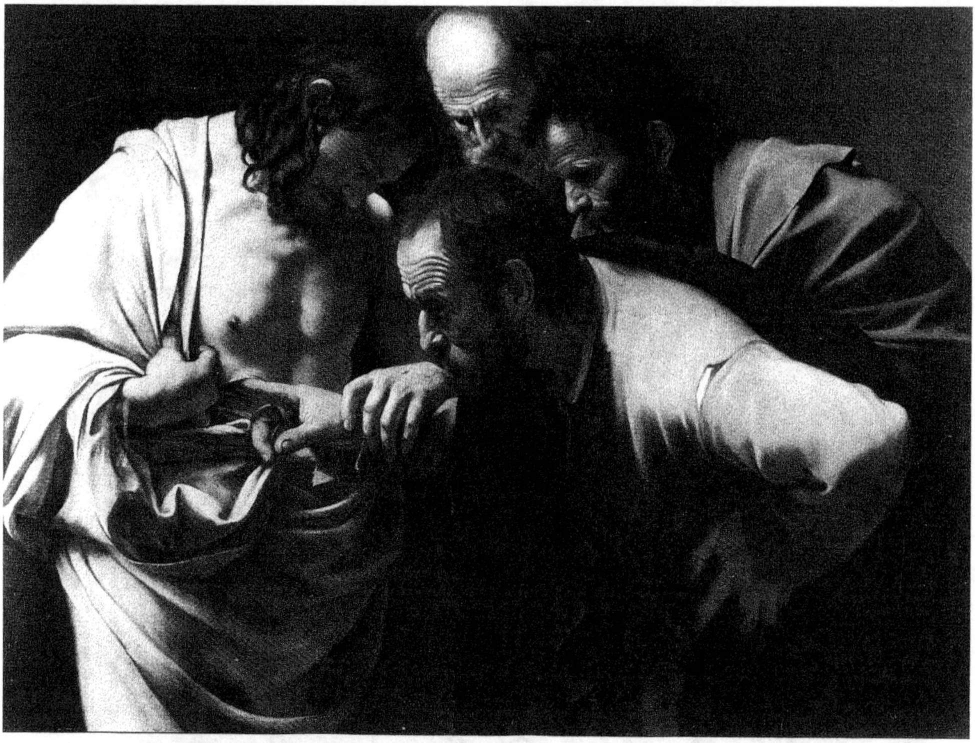

(*above*) Caravaggio (attrib.) (1573–1610), *Doubting Thomas* (Neues Palais, Potsdam).

(*below*) Rembrandt (1606–69), *Bathsheba* (1654) (Louvre, Paris).

3 Rembrandt, *Abraham and Isaac* (1635) (The Hermitage, St Petersburg; The Mansell Collection).

4 Rembrandt, *The Risen Christ appearing to the Magdalen* (1638) (Her Majesty the Queen).

5 Gustav Klimt (1862–1918), *The Kiss* (1907–8) (Österreichische Galerie, Vienna).

6

Living in the Reel World: The Bible in Film

It is extraordinary how quickly film attracted theoretical, and indeed, philosophical attention. In a remarkable passage in his book of 1911 on evolutionary theory, *Creative Evolution*, the French philosopher Henri Bergson analyses what he describes as the "cinematographical method". That is, the way in which a film takes a series of static images and unrolls them in continuous sequence so "that each actor of the scene recovers his mobility".[1] Linking the contrivance of the cinematograph with that of our knowledge, Bergson describes it as a reconstitution of "the individuality of each particular movement by combining his nameless movement with the personal attitudes". The movement exists, but it is only in the apparatus of the cinema and its techniques, an artificial recomposition of "becoming".

In the medieval world, also, the notion of change in organic beings was one of the substitution of one static form for another in a series of sequences. Thus, today, the cinema re-creates and "frames" the biblical narratives through the interpretative technology of the screen, from reel to reel, assuming a high degree of the willing suspension of disbelief in the audience/reader. The static image is recomposed in the apparatus of the film, artificially, as a realization of the medieval notion of change, in the form of an illusion.

There have been two films made with the title *King of Kings*, one in black and white, silent, directed in 1927 by Cecil B. De Mille. It was the most expensive silent picture ever made, and as a merely visual experience demands a degree of contributory participation on the part of the audience – a greater contribution to its reel-ality – than the later talking picture. There, the danger of the claims of a naive "realism" are greater and, perhaps ultimately, less persuasive. The second *King of Kings* was directed by Nicholas Ray in 1961 with all the visual benefits of what was then known as "super Technirama", and advertised as delivering "the glory of Christ's spoken words". Of the two, Cecil B. De Mille's is easily the better, indeed it is something of a classic partly because it so daringly diverges from any pretence at biblical accuracy, being a life of Jesus seen more or less from the viewpoint of Mary Magdalen. Its fantasy is far more bizarre than anything proposed by Michèle Roberts in *The Wild Girl*, Mary inhabiting a luxurious palace apparently infested with zebras, in total disregard of any notion of reference to the texts of the gospels. It is so absurd in its brilliant fantasy one almost has to take it seriously when, as if by accident, moments such as the exorcism of demons from Mary in a swirl of ghostly figures, technically extraordinary for its day, become dramatically highly effective. More hilarious touches are crowned by the, now famous, sub-titled command: "Harness my zebras, gift of the Nubian king!"

The history of the cinema is littered with the wreckage of worthy attempts to translate the Bible into film, anxious and often devout experiments, as it were, to overcome the anxiety expressed in Jorge Luis Borges's "parable", "Paradiso XXXI, 108":

> Men have lost face, an irrecoverable face, and all long to be that pilgrim (envisioned in the Empyrean beneath the Rose) who in Rome sees the Veronica and faithfully murmurs: "My Lord, Jesus Christ, true God, and was this, then, the fashion of thy semblance?"
>
> There is a stone face beside a road with an inscription saying "The True Portrait of the Holy Face of the God of Jaen": if we really knew what it was like, the key to all the parables would be ours and we would know if the carpenter's son was also the Son of God.[2]

The cinema, perhaps even more insistently than the art of painting, seems to hold out the possibility of "true representation", a genuine mimesis which enables the viewer to walk beside the Christ himself and participate visually in the narrative of his life. Most, though not all, of this chapter will be concerned with the idea of Jesus Christ as a movie star, and with the moving/speaking image of the film as interpreter of biblical narratives within the canonical tradition. The screen interests me, in the first place simply because one recognizes immediately there the experience of *limitation* and *deception*. I illustrate what I mean at its extreme from an amusing (and utterly serious) memorandum, "Hints for television broadcasters", written in 1931 by William Schudt of CBS:

> ACTION is a very important factor in visual broadcasting. It has been found that an active image comes through more clearly

> than any others. Act as much as possible in your program. Use your hands, head, and shoulders – also, where songs indicate, roll your eyes, and shake your finger at the televisor.
>
> While broadcasting you may move around in a TWO FOOT SQUARE SPACE without getting out of focus. Look into the light to either side of it. DO NOT LOOK up at the microphone.
>
> If you move out of the picture, the production man will give you a light tap or push you in the right direction. When such corrections are made, try not to look around in an amazed manner. Lookers-in will be quick to notice the unpremeditated move.[3]

The magic of film and television is, to its very core, a *deceiver's* art, an art of acting and illusion. Assuming a high level of literacy in its viewers who must learn – as one "learns" to read – to accept the screen's framing and lineality without protest, the cinema demands and plays upon sophisticated techniques of interpretation and reception. I confess that the production man mentioned in this memorandum seems to me to resemble very closely the biblical critic who is anxious to bring a scriptural character to life by imposing on the text the conditions of critical methodologies which enable the figure to "act" – but the moment it moves out of critical focus it receives a slight tap or push to keep it in the TWO FOOT SQUARE SPACE of orthodoxy and acceptability, unconcerned and never quite looking straight ahead. As in the Hollywood biblical epic, a great deal of effort is expended in convincing the reader/viewer of historical verisimilitude and accuracy. Yet one is always suspicious that biblical criticism tends to reflect more of its *own* time than any "biblical era". Even more blatantly, Cecil B. De Mille engaged in lengthy and detailed "historical research" in the making of his film *The Ten Commandments* (1956), but ends up saying far more about the United States in the mid-twentieth century than anything else.

Yet it is the very ability of art, and not least the art of the cinema, successfully to deceive which can make it so worryingly subversive, if also creative in its attention to the Bible. Hal Ashby's 1979 film of Jerzy Kosinski's novel *Being There* (a satiric novel and film which are saturated with facetious transfigurations of the Jesus narrative) is partly an exploration of both the mysterious power and falsity of a life which has lost the ability to distinguish between the television image and the "real world". The simple gardener brilliantly played by Peter Sellers, whose only name is Chance, knows the world only through television, which he watches obsessively – cartoons, news, films, advertisements, quiz shows, children's programmes, all making equal and unquestioned claims upon him. Chance's repeated phrase "I like to watch", renders him literally impotent, unable to interpret the politics of Washington D.C., sexual and otherwise, which whirl around him. As one commentator describes it, "What borders on the absurd at the level of superficial visual realism makes profound sense at the level of the film's expressionistic meaning: it is the mind that is left limp by the experience."[4]

But the expressionistic juxtaposition of narrative continuity and media commentary which lies at the heart of the film of *Being There* repeatedly emphasizes the interplay of incommensurates which comprises its satire and its exposure. For Chance – Chauncey Gardener – is the innocent impotent text which exposes every wily, intriguing political and sexual interpretation. At the beginning of the film he is, quite literally, innocence expelled from the garden, where he has laboured, witlessly and cut off from the world outside, all his life. Like the stereotype which Chaplin discovered at the heart of the illusion of film, most brilliantly perhaps in *Modern Times*, Chaplin's last silent picture into which he also introduces expressionist sound techniques, Chance surpasses the "real life" of Washington D.C. which he exposes by his illusory world: the key, as Marshall McLuhan puts it "to the pathos of a mechanized civilisation".[5] At the end of the film, finally, he walks away across the lake, in a familiar biblical image, which simply invalidates the "serious" political intrigue which focuses upon his central, still, almost silent absurdity.

Being There employs the same devices as the English medieval miracle plays, as they emerged from the Church's liturgy, and eventually earned them its hostility. In them is found the almost silent Christ, a figure around whom whirls the sometimes comic, sometimes tragic drama, a figure representing a limitlessness judging the intrigues of the politics of time. The effect of the dramatic shift to the play of linear time and localized space in the emergence of Christian drama from Christian rite is described by O. B. Hardison Jr, in his now classic study of the origin and early history of modern drama:

> Ritual action occurs in the context of the timeless present and unlocalized space. At the moment of the Mass sacrifice, past, present and future are one, and the congregation is united with Christians everywhere in the mystical body of Christ. Liturgical

drama represents the first sustained crossing of the boundary between ritual and representation in the Middle Ages.[6]

It is the repeated failure of modern cinema's versions of the "Life of Christ" to recognize this intersection which dooms so many of its attempts to failure. Indeed, the cinema, in its popular Hollywood version at least, has been hopelessly inept at recognizing the nature of its involvement in traditions of representation and theory of mimesis at all. The too-serious refusal to risk the comedy of the intersection of liturgical ritual and dramatic representation – or, if you prefer more simply, the eternal and the temporal – results merely in absurdity, a wrong packaging of the deceiver's art, so that John Wayne's classic moment in George Stevens's film *The Greatest Story Ever Told* (1965), as the centurion drawling awe-fully at the foot of the Cross, "Truly this man was the Son of God", becomes an act of hilarious inappropriateness. Art, as we know, must tell it slant, thus Chance, the gardener, becoming a deliciously effective and facetious transfiguration of Jesus. As one film critic remarked: "God is unlucky in *The Greatest Story Ever Told*. His only begotten son turns out to be a bore . . . the photography is inspired mainly by Hallmark Cards."[7] John Wayne, unwittingly, becomes the hero of those serious biblical critics who nudge their scriptural characters into the two foot square *sitz im leben* of their historical and theological obsessions. It is Chauncey Gardener, the unlikely, impotent subversive of *Being There,* who is liturgically and dramatically simply "there" between reality and unreality, and recalls us to the uncomfortable, largely unread *literacy* of the Bible narratives: who, like Christ, is simply there in the midst of things, unmoved (the pathetic, helpless figure at the heart of the passion play who admits, "I am very thirsty"), and tests the depth of the lake on which he walks with his umbrella, for all the world like Stan Laurel. While the politics of the world continue their talkative machinations, in the final scene of the film, Chauncey returns to his tending of the trees and innocently walks off across the water in a brilliant moment of comedy which casts a beam back across the whole narrative of the film, back to its beginnings in the innocence of the garden.

There is the real subversion of cinematic deception, in a character unconsciously deconstructing the false narratives of the screen – the cartoons and the newsreels which bind our decisions, yet which are expelled by our hermeneutics – embodying, like the biblical narratives, the fundamental perception that our living before God takes place both outside time and space, and yet also inextricably bound within these transforming media, incessantly and always in relationships with others.[8]

Unconsciously the medium of film, through its natural surrealism and violence, may rehearse the natural surrealism and violence of the biblical narrative, and in particular the narrative of the gospels.[9] The *theological* misunderstanding of the *art* of biblical narrative (that is, as was suggested in the previous chapter, its *literary* counter-coherence to theological configuration) is well expressed by Friedrich Nietzsche in an early writing, "On Truth and Lies in a Nonmoral Sense", where he notes that art "treats illusion as *illusion:* therefore it does not wish to deceive; it is *true*".[10] In so far as art is an illusion whose only truth is that it is an illusion, art is only true as a lie. When the illusion of art is mistaken for truth, art is destroyed.

That is why the most "successful" screen "lives of Christ" are those which employ fictional transfigurations of Jesus, or which work through a self-conscious theatrical motif like the 1989 French Canadian film *Jesus of Montreal,* or, perhaps most seriously of all, the 1979 *Monty Python's Life of Brian,* a film to which I will return in due course.

The sense of the lying truth of the cinema – beautifully crafted in the film parable of Kosinski's *Being There* – takes me back to Jacques Derrida's review of his teacher Michel Foucault in this 1963 lecture "Cogito and the History of Madness", and in particular Derrida's personal sense of discipleship. Forgive me a longish but necessary quotation:

> Now, the disciple's consciousness, when he starts, I would not say to dispute, but to engage in dialogue with the master or, better, to articulate the interminable and silent dialogue which made him into a disciple – this disciple's consciousness is an unhappy consciousness. Starting to enter into dialogue in the world, that is, starting to answer back, he always feels "caught in the act", like the "infant" who, by definition and as his name indicates, cannot speak and above all must not answer back. And when, as is the case here, the dialogue is in danger of being taken – incorrectly – as a challenge, the disciple knows that he alone finds himself already challenged by the master's voice within him that precedes his own. He feels himself indefinitely challenged, or rejected or accused; as a disciple, he is challenged by the master who speaks within him and before him, to reproach

> him for making this challenge and to reject it in advance, having elaborated it before him; and having interiorized the master, he is also challenged by the disciple that he himself is. This interminable unhappiness of the disciple perhaps stems from the fact that he does not yet know – or is still concealing from himself – that the master, like real life, may always be absent. The disciple must break the glass, or better the mirror, the reflection, his infinite speculation on the master. And start to speak.[11]

This deeply personal reflection on discipleship and the master–servant relationship and the absent master should be compulsory reading for all would-be directors of film "lives of Christ". It raises the question of dialogue and its difficulty – the *trauma* of maintaining a conversation with the master who both dominates and, being absent, refuses to answer. An attitude of pious subjection may not, in fact, reflect proper discipleship or maturity. That is, of course, always fraught with danger. Later in this same essay, Derrida characterizes philosophy as "perhaps the reassurance given against the anguish of being mad at the point of greatest proximity to madness" (p. 59). Philosophy – or more broadly we might say critical orthodoxy – restrains and *denies* that "voice" of the philosophic disciple which necessarily both continues and undermines the philosophical tradition – another version, perhaps, of the sense in poetic theory of the anxiety of influence. As Stanley Cavell, who originally directed me to Derrida's words, – philosopher and film critic – expresses it, "being gifted pupils, they seem to accept and to assassinate with the same gesture".[12]

That, it seems to me, is not a bad description of Jesus's attitude to "the tradition" in the gospels: "I did not come to abolish but to complete" (Matthew 5: 17); "I tell you this: not one stone will be left upon another; all will be thrown down" (Matthew 24: 2).

Seeing Jesus as disciple – Jesus beginning to "write" (as Stephen Moore might put it) – is to assert the voice which "orthodoxy" and its denial of writing serves to suppress: that is, Jesus as "text" which we now only assess by a reading process and not by orality – Jesus as effect, the founder in the written and visual "word". The film which claims to present "the glory" of Christ's spoken words forgets that these words are always mediated through the experience of others – his disciples and apostles –, and the pen of the evangelist. What we see in such films as the 1961 *King of Kings* is the gloomy and infinitely tedious face of our own "infinite speculation on the master". As Derrida perceived, the interminable unhappiness of such films stems from the fact that they conceal from themselves that the master, like real life, may always be absent.

How does one then overcome this denial of voice so that the disciple, and therefore the master, may start to speak, overcoming the madness of a tedious sanity? The lesson which the too-loving Peter learned with such difficulty, that the master must be allowed to serve us, has to be learned. One begins by recognizing the chiasma of the master as servant, and thereby give the servant voice: by recognizing the wisdom of the fools – the Chauncey Gardeners – which may be wiser than men. One recalls, in film that our only view of the Master is through the writings and reflections of his disciples, from which a rather dull, magisterial prototype has been abstracted. Instead, the master/servant must learn to speak with his challenging voice. The master himself becomes the servant who speaks. Films which uncomfortably brush against religious self-satisfaction may be the ones that matter in the end, their tactics, consciously or unconsciously, related to the proposals of Stephen D. Moore's recent poststructuralist study of Mark and Luke. He writes there:

> I am eager to reply to the Gospels in kind, to write in a related idiom. Rather than take a jackhammer to the concrete, parabolic language of the Gospels, replacing graphic images with abstract categories, I prefer to respond to a pictographic text pictographically, to a narrative text narratively, producing a critical text that is a postmodern analogue of the premodern text that it purports to read.[13]

Films which respond in this way "in kind" to the Gospels, I suggest, are *Jesus of Montreal* and *Monty Python's Life of Brian*. Why so? Each refuses to offer a "straight" image of Jesus, but rather, exploiting the cinema's art of surrealism and deception, they grant a "voice" to Jesus (like the gospels) through the textuality of the "play within the play" (*Jesus of Montreal*) and satirical comedy revue (*Life of Brian*). Each, like *Being There*, looks back to the medieval drama, in the theatrical mode of the passion play.

In *Jesus of Montreal* a rather down-at-heel group of young actors and actresses perform a passion play in the grounds of a Montreal monastery. Their backgrounds are, to say the least, dubious. One has been employed as a voice-over in pornographic movies. Another has been exploited as a model in advertising, using her body to sell products. A third is the lover of one of the Roman Catholic priests. They are gathered together by the "Jesus" character, who writes and directs their play, himself an outcast. They enact a radical revision of a tedious liturgical dramatic tradition in the community, which incurs the wrath of the ecclesiastical authorities. Simple in structure, and occasionally falling into banality (notably the "overturning" of the exploitative theatre director's electronic equipment in a moment of gospel parody), the film nevertheless sustains a sense – looking back especially to Luke's Gospel – of "Jesus" as the object of blindness or insight, reading or misreading. Indeed "readings" occur throughout the film, in attempts to perceive the true nature of "role". In Luke's Gospel, Jesus, looking back to the text of Isaiah, begins his ministry in the Nazareth synagogue (4: 16ff.) with an act of self-reading which is also the act of an ideal reader of scripture. In *Jesus of Montreal*, the central character who plays Jesus writes the text of the play – *is* the Jesus who begins to write, to write *himself*, that is. But in each case, and increasingly in the film, his own identity is almost illegible, unreadable, though effecting release for others from blindness, oppression, exploitation. Finally his body is used to give life to others through medical transplants.

Stephen Moore reminds us that in Luke's Gospel the congregation's initial response to Jesus's words, of stunned amazement, is described in their "gaze" – the Greek "ἀτενίζω" having the connotation here, as in Acts 3: 12, of misrecognition. In Luke 4: 20, the synagogue crowd fix an uncomprehending gaze upon him: they look without perception.

Jesus, as ideal reader, also lets scripture read him (Luke 4: 21) and this is precisely what his congregation will not or cannot do; that is – *read*. In the film, I suggest, we both read and do not read: that is, we are given the uncomfortable possibility of the role of the disciple – to accept and to assassinate, to read and to misread. I do not think I am claiming too much for the film, which has many faults. Its appropriation by Christian fundamentalists has been a matter of deep concern to its director – not surprisingly. It works in so far as it exploits the deceptive, dramatic, surreal and subversive qualities of the medium and succeeds, therefore, as an intertext, pictographically and narratively, and not merely an abstraction from the gospel narratives.

And *The Life of Brian*? Here I will be very brief. On its release in

1979 it evoked howls of protest from churches, and was frequently banned from screenings. But it was, its creators insisted, not an attack on the Christian faith, rather a satire on their own experience of English public school religion and the practices of Christianity and biblical critics. With wicked historical "accuracy" the Sermon on the Mount takes place on a Saturday afternoon – about teatime. The hermeneutical problems of "hearing" a discourse across the temporal abyss of two thousand years of history are parodied in the device of using the spatial problem of listeners at the back of the crowd who are simply too far away from the speaker to catch his words clearly. Brian, the central character, is continually mistaken for the Jesus of the gospels, and in a curious way, is very similar to the Christs of the medieval passion plays. He plays his part beautifully, and finally almost silently, and is the object of continual misreadings. The point in the end is that Brian *is* Christ precisely in so far as he is misunderstood and his identity mistaken. The essential comedy of the film draws directly upon the medieval tradition of literature which lampoons corrupt ecclesiastical practices, with stock comic figures drawn from contemporary life. And it is, paradoxically, the film's theatrical motif which forces the audience into the uncomfortable "scriptural" exercise of reading/misreading. For as Martin Scorsese, the director of *The Last Temptation* remarked, the difficulty with his *direct* presentation of the figure of Christ is that audiences simply do not listen. Perhaps it is the old problem of "ἀτενίζω": the gaze which refuses to read, and eventually simply casts the intruder out. One needs to read obliquely, and against the grain.

The difference between Scorsese's film and *The Life of Brian*, one a high budget Hollywood movie by an undeniably fine film director, the other little more than a series of satirical sketches, is that the latter does, paradoxically, give the central increasingly silent figure a voice: in Derrida's words of the disciple, he starts to speak. It is a recognition, perhaps, of that profound *fictionality* – albeit historical fictionality – of the gospels and scriptural narratives, picked up in the subversion of cinematic deception.

The once-popular genre of the Hollywood biblical epic has become now the subject not of curiosity about the Bible, but of studies of the American culture which portrayed its own images of itself in the guise of the salvation narratives of scripture. Charlton Heston as Moses, John Huston as Noah – are American stereotypes in a society which clearly saw itself in the role of saving the world. As one reviewer wittily and perceptively remarked of De Mille's absurd epic *Samson and Delilah* (1949):

> Perhaps de Mille's survival is due to the fact that he decided in his movie nonage to ally himself with God as his co-maker and get his major scripts from the Bible, which he has always handled with the proprietary air of a gentleman fondling old love-letters.[14]

One begins to feel that the Hollywood glamour of a Cecil B. De Mille Hollywood epic and the textually anxious researchings of the official "history of religion" may not, after all, be so far apart. Each has got into a muddle of self-perception, not to say projection.

It has been remarked that foreign film imports were once very popular in Thailand, partly as a result of a peculiar technique of overcoming the difficulty of foreign languages, a technique known as "Adam and Eving".[15] The Thai dialogue was articulated as the film was run by Thai actors speaking through a loudspeaker while hidden from the audience. The technique demanded great skill and endurance, and was, apparently, highly paid. The actors were, we might say, formalizing what we all subconsciously do while watching the screen: interpolating our own interpretation during the tedious exchanges of the film gods and goddesses.

The greatest films of familiar "biblical" narratives precisely and obliquely engineer their own fictionality – in expressionist manner present a narrative of images: the pathetic and redemptive Chaplin clown, the mysterious stranger of *Shane* or Eastwood's *High Plains Drifter*, the confused, innocent Brian – all characters who step into "our" world yet move uneasily or menacingly in the flickering world "up there" on the screen. Yet they remain obtusely "other", mysteriously present yet absent in a different dimension. The screen preserves its own gods and goddesses for us to "read", and we see all too often the human tragedies which ensue when actors and actresses are forced to bear the burden of this divinity into their own lives. Like Heller's King David, they become pathetic, overburdened beings, human, all too human. Perhaps they serve to remind us that such burdens are more than mere humanity can tolerate: they give us a new sense of the kaleidoscope of scripture.

Woody Allen's bittersweet comedy of the Great Depression, *The Purple Rose of Cairo* (1984), explores the cinema's uneasy relationship with "reality", and the mayhem which ensues when a screen hero steps into the wrong dimension, when dreams become "real". In the written text of the gospels, as in the textuality of the cinema, the life of Christ remains powerful in the interpretative energy of reading and accommodation and our willing suspension of disbelief in faith. Theological reality depends, it may be said, upon a return to Bergson's cinematographical methods – as he describes it:

> Each of our acts aim at a certain insertion of our will into the reality. There is, between our body and other bodies, an arrangement like that of the pieces of glass that compose a kaleidoscopic picture. Our activity goes from an arrangement to a rearrangement, each time no doubt giving the kaleidoscope a new shake, but not interesting itself in the shake, and seeing only the new picture. Our knowledge of the operation of nature must be exactly symmetrical, therefore, with the interest we take in our own operation. In this sense we may say, if we are not abusing this kind of illustration, that *the cinematographical character of our knowledge of things is due to the kaleidoscopic character of our adaptation to them.*[16]

Notes

1. Henri Bergson, *Creative Evolution*, trans. Arthur Mitchell (London, 1911) pp. 321–3. See also Marshall McLuhan, *Understanding Media: The Extensions of Man* (1964; London, 1987) ch. 29: "Movies: the Reel World", pp. 284–96. More generally for this chapter, see also Bruce Babington and Peter William Evans, *Biblical Epics: Sacred Narrative in the Hollywood Cinema* (Manchester, 1993).
2. Jorge Juis Borges, *Labyrinths: Selected Stories and Other Writings*, ed. Donald A. Yates and James E. Irby (Harmondsworth, 1970) p. 274.
3. Quoted in William Boddy, "'Spread like a monster blanket over the country': CBS and television, 1929–33", *Screen*, vol. 32 (1991) 178–9.
4. John R. May, "The New Generation of American Directors and Cinema's Subversive Art", in Robert Detweiler (ed.), *Art/Literature/Religion: Life on the Borders*, JAAR Thematic Studies 49/2 (Chico, 1983) p. 113.
5. McLuhan, *Understanding Media*, p. 290.
6. O. B. Hardison Jr, *Christian Rite and Christian Drama in the Middle Ages* (Baltimore, 1965) p. 271.

7. John Simon, quoted in *Halliwell's Film Guide*, 7th edn (London, 1989) p. 428.
8. See also Robert Alter, *The Art of Biblical Narrative* (London, 1981) p. 22.
9. See Stanley Cavell, "Naughty Orators: Negation of Voice in *Gaslight*", in Sanford Budick and Wofgang Iser (eds), *Languages of the Unsayable* (New York, 1989) p. 357.
10. Friedrich Nietzsche, *Philosophy and Truth: Selections from Nietzsche's Notebooks*, trans. and ed. David Breazeale (New Jersey, 1979) p. 84. See, further, Irena Makarushka, "Decomposing the American Dream: the Ambiguity of Evil in *Blue Velvet*", *Religion and American Culture*, vol. I (1991) 31–46.
11. Jacques Derrida, "Cogito and the History of Madness", in *Writing and Difference*, trans. Alan Bass (London, 1978) pp. 31–63, esp. pp. 31–2.
12. Cavell, "Naughty Orators", p. 363, quoting from S. Cavell, *Must We Mean What We Say?: A Book of Essays* (Cambridge, 1976) p. 21, n. 19. See also Harold Bloom, *The Anxiety of Influence: A Theory of Poetry* (Oxford, 1973).
13. Stephen D. Moore, *Mark and Luke in Poststructuralist Perspectives* (New Haven, Conn., 1992) p. xviii.
14. *New Yorker*, in *Halliwell's Film Guide*, p. 879.
15. See McLuhan, *Understanding Media*, p. 296.
16. Bergson, *Creative Evdution*, p. 323.

7

Violence and Postmodernism: Is There No Hope in the Evil Demon of Images?

"Postmodernism" is a word so frequently used and so little clearly understood that its very lack of stable reference could be said to justify the notion of a condition known as "postmodern". In *The Postmodern Condition* of 1979, Jean-François Lyotard suggests this definition of the word:

> [postmodernism] designates the state of our culture following the transformations which, since the end of the nineteenth century, have altered the game rules for science, literature, and the arts.[1]

These paradigm shifts, which, I would claim, culture has barely begun even to recognize, Lyotard characterizes as states of *crisis,* that is, crisis not merely as a way of thinking about "the moment" but a condition of chaos inherent in the moment itself. (For the opposite view, see below p. 111). Such postmodern thinking looks back to Friedrich Nietzsche, with his proclamation of the death of God and his prophecy in *The Will to Power* of a new dark age which would be typified by *passive nihilists,* driven by despair over their own bungled instincts toward predatory behaviour, and by *suicidal nihilists,* who always prefer to will nothingness rather than not will at all.[2] In his writing and in his insane life, Nietzsche exemplifies the radical isolation of the postmodern.

Instability and indeterminacy of language and image characterize the postmodern, which is at best, perhaps, the image that there is no image of the whole of things.[3] Yet this very semantic indeterminacy may oddly serve to sustain a religious fundamentalism that is the cavalier appropriation of the "sacred" text to support a religious system even in defiance of its sense or potential meaning.[4]

To my mind somewhat chillingly, the Anglican theologian Stephen Sykes can acknowledge what he describes as "modern uncertainty", in the face of which he proposes not a careful, painful critical exercise in reading and ethical exploration, but the theological imposition of power within the institution which has appropriated the canon of scripture. Thus he writes in *The Identity of Christianity*:

> One of the themes of the book concerns the responsibility of the Christian theologian in his [*sic*] exercise of power in the church, a power which resides in his or her articulacy, or power to communicate. I hold that a theologian must communicate to other than fellow theologians and that clarification of meaning is one of the few justifications for occupying time and money in the production and reading of works of scholarship.[5]

The huge assumptions made here regarding the possibility of communication, meaning and power, become deeply offensive in the face of the postmodern critique, actually demonic as the wielding of that which has lost all ethical validity even, or maybe especially, within the tradition which is still prepared to give credence to such authority. In the postmodern world we face the terrible isolation which ensues when that power which had seemed to make things possible for us – the power of Sykes's theologian – is unmasked and an unthinkable apocalypse is revealed. As Michel Foucault acknowledged:

> power is only tolerable on the condition that it masks a considerable part of itself. Its success is proportional to its ability to hide its own mechanisms . . . secrecy . . . is indispensable to its operation.[6]

This secrecy, as it is exercised in the canon of the Bible, is what I have been seeking to expose in the images of art and literature which lie outside the institutional integration of power relationships worked out in the pages of the sacred text. Such masking is motivated, no doubt, in large part by that *nostalgia* which Derrida calls in Heidegger a "desire to recover the proper name, the unique name of Being", and which Sykes continues to identify in Christianity's original nature "as something simple, clear and imaginative, capable of appealing to the unlettered".[7]

Given the nature of Heidegger's own political exposure, the danger of such nostalgia is self-evident. But what is the nature of resistance within postmodernity to such deeply engrained attractions? My response to that question should be apparent from the preceding chapters of this book. For my part, there is a need to move outside the "funded Christian theological tradition"[8] into a condition of "interdisciplinarity" – that is reading this tradition against the grain of its orthodoxies. But, as Stanley Fish once pointed out, "being interdisciplinary is so very hard to do".[9] Nevertheless, "the impossibility of authentic critique is the impossibility of the interdisciplinary project". How do we set about this impossibility?

Abandoning nostalgia, which is ultimately a condition of violence, we must think within the interdisciplinarity of intertextuality in a self-sacrifice which articulates the unsayable and thinks the unthinkable. To live the life of such authentic thought will be a terrible burden in the face of the necessary evil of writing, unsustained by the claims of any moment of naive purity at its root. Any such articulation is only made possible by the unarticulated ground within which it occurs, a violation of violence, dangerously releasing the evil demon of images. As we read of the often nameless victims of scripture, those whose tragedies are so often revealed in the imagination and drama of art, we learn shamelessly to "misread" those texts which threaten to dominate us by their orthodoxy in the tradition.

One must use the word "misread" with care. While it may be true to say that any reading is a misreading (a comment without much value), is there not an ethical demand, at least, that our encounters with textuality are motivated not by the desire for definition or the exercise of power but, as Emmanuel Levinas might put it, by an endless obligation to the other, "a multiplicity in being which refuses totalization and takes form instead as a fraternity and discourse, an ethical relation which forever precedes and exceeds the egoism and tyranny of ontology".[10] Such an activity Levinas proposes over against the demands of "the avaricious, power-seeking, organizing, self-same self".[11]

Yet, in this provocative, self-consciously "postmodern" activity, do we not ourselves become the perpetrators of a postmodern violence, or, at least, responsible for the exposure of an apocalypticism to which we have no response beyond a nihilistic nightmare? Is there now no place for the notion of salvation?

Of course this fear which has come upon us is not new in literature and art. When John Milton composed *Paradise Lost*, his fellow poet Andrew Marvell, as we have seen, feared that such a massive assault upon the scriptural story of Adam and Eve would be a "ruin" of "sacred Truths": in the event, Marvell concluded that Milton had in fact preserved the canonical writings "inviolate".[12] Yet the suspicion of textual violation continues to haunt Milton criticism from Dr Johnson in the eighteenth century to William Empson nearer our own time: Milton, unwittingly of the devil's party.

Or, in art, as we have seen, Rembrandt continually transgresses the biblical text in a constant visual violation of narrative order, reversing of priorities, extension of significance. Stories and episodes trigger images which move beyond their theological and literary parentage. Rembrandt – the postmodern?

Hardly; yet the violent seeds are there, presented in the breaking of the biblical images, even as they are offered in the images of literature and art: images which affront the violence of conformity, saying the unsayable, thinking the unthinkable. In the postmodern condition this entails a final abandonment of the mimetic tradition, as of logocentricity, in an apocalypse which may serve to reveal instead the evil demon of images themselves in the iconography of an age of nihilism. The subject of the next chapter will be this contemporary apocalyptic, enquiring whether there is actually nothing after a bleak vision of the violence of self-destruction. Is this the only possible consequence of a revealing of the powers of canonical order? Here, suffice it to suggest that the apocalypse of the postmodern has, indeed, its grammar, though exhibited in violence and absurdity. It may, paradoxically (even religiously) be a learning to *say* the unsayable. That, of course, must always be deeply painful, any movement towards the codification of points of resistance which make revolution possible dangerously mimicking – or perhaps parodying – the prior institutional integration of the relationships of power in a narrative of "salvation" and conformity. But while in the art of biblical narrative we find divine order, typological linkage or ultimate control in our *reading* of events, the postmodern on the other hand offers a sense of the provisional and arbitrary nature of narratives in a scatalogical, absurd fantasy world which is either profoundly creative or finally destructive. Space and time become relative in texts which religiously/irreligiously celebrate the absolute otherness of God, a supreme fiction at best, ludicrously real or seriously invented, in his "death" the instigation of all paradigm shifts.

It was Jean Baudrillard who coined the term the "evil demon of images" in his 1984 Mari Kuttna Memorial lecture on Film in the University of Sydney. Before we dispense with this demon which has been let loose, and consider possible grounds for the recovery of the sacred in scripture, we need to take wholly seriously its demonism in the deep perversity of Baudrillard's vision. At best we might begin to exercise what Georges Bataille has described as a "hypermorality" – an acute and often painful awareness of the radical evil at the heart of the human condition and its systems of control – which may be all that is granted us in the panic of the *fin-de-millenium* mood of contemporary culture.[13]

We have seen how literature, art and the cinema have exploded the carefully, canonically controlled images of the Bible in a carnival of images, a Menippean discourse in literature suggesting a form and thought similar to that of painting: that is, "the configuration of (literary) space as revealing (literary) thought without 'realist' pretensions".[14] Postmodernity shifts the nightmare into a higher gear of cultural amnesia, beyond even nostalgia, into a hyper-pessimism which thrills to catastrophe and implodes ecstatically into excess and waste. Baudrillard's nihilism is anticipated by Walter Benjamin in his remarks on the dreadful inversion of the mimetic tradition in the images of the age of mechanical reproduction:

> It is precisely when it appears most truthful, most faithful and most in conformity to reality that the image is most diabolical – and our technical images, whether they be from photography, cinema or television, are in the overwhelming majority much more "figurative", "realist", than all the images from past cultures. It is in its resemblance, not only analogical but technological, that the image is most immoral and most perverse.[15]

We have become the victims of the massive and seductive con-trick of the image, perverting the tradition and its narratives with which we have been concerned. Has all been in vain – the shift between stability and adaptability which has been observed in the life and revival of the Bible in ever-new forms of art and re-presentation? What is under threat in Benjamin's essay is the work of art itself – with its lively voice of challenge to the dead hand of traditional reading – in the age of the mechanic.

Here Baudrillard sees a new and deadly form of the apocalyptic vision, a "diabolical conformity" in image making, which finds a correspondence in sociological, historical and political experience,[16] effectively blocking the liberating qualities of art, the politics of feminism, the "scriptures" of modern fiction. What is lost in the age of mechanical reproduction is individuality – what is ever-present is conformism masquerading as the unique, the individual, the special. Hence, we find in postmodernity an endless plurality of interpretations available, precisely because at no point can one stop and say, "that's it": the power of the image resides in its endless resistance to definition, its endless refusal of the responsibility "to be". Baudrillard draws a comparison between the Vietnam war, and Francis Ford Coppola's film *Apocalypse Now* as an image of the war perceived as "the heart of darkness".[17] Which is the "real" war – each, Vietnam and the film, being a celebration of American technology, neither culminating in any adequate conclusion? The image and its "reality" merge, without any sense of critical distance or raising of consciousness. We cannot afford that in our age of panic, for reality cannot be borne – as in Dostoevsky's *Brothers Karamozov,* we *need* our grand inquisitors to protect us from truths which cannot be endured. But the demons have removed from us a sense of "reality" which alone can guarantee discernment, legitimation and responsible action.

The demon images – of the screen, of our contemporary "myths" – have *become* our reality. We live in a postmodern world of simulacra which bear their own stunning logic. Order has been reversed, a chain reaction *backwards*. Yet we blatantly fail to see that anything is fundamentally amiss, so that, as Baudrillard observes:

> we all remain incredibly naive: we always look for a good usage, without seeing that the image in a sense revolts against this good usage, that it is the conductor neither of meaning nor good intentions, but on the contrary of an implosion, a denigration of meaning (of events, history, memory, etc.).[18]

Baudrillard is writing specifically of the "postmodern" images of the television and cinema screens. But may we not, even more, apply his insights to the images which traditionally sustain our sense of the Bible as the Good Book, written for our salvation – images which govern the narratives of our liturgies, creeds and confessions? Have these simply come to contribute to the overwhelming thrill of catastrophe and the consumerism at the heart of our anti-social inertia:[19] an apocalypse without hope?

The image which flickers on the screen of our imagination then becomes the only "reality", the final solution (a deathly, genocidal term) to the historical quest which has haunted Christian theology and biblical interpretation in the past two centuries, the only guarantor of the historicity of any event. The translation of an "event" (like the Holocaust) into an image – a process familiar enough in theology and liturgical practice – far from performing an exorcism, entertains and multiplies the demons and perpetuates their being in an event which is tolerated because it is after all "only" an image. In Marshall McLuhan's well-worn phrase, "the medium is the message". But, if this is so, the image is not merely an image, it is all we know of "the thing itself", and thus it is inoffensive to our imagination, which has died. Thus we spiral into the ecstasy of final incoherency, and the narratives of salvation are robbed of any teleological possibility by the endless succession of "repeats". The introduction of the video film is the ultimate expression of this. The same "event" can be experienced endlessly, whenever we wish; we can rewind and repeat, in slow motion or in reverse, or we can stop time altogether in the frozen frame. Time becomes meaningless, the moment or καιρός endlessly deferred or indulged in, while all sense of "the real" is wilfully set aside. We no longer even desire to bear the responsibility of it.

As Baudrillard points out, there is a collusion between images and life which concludes finally in an implosion of image and reality. The images which have *sustained* our traditions of reading scripture and belief, and which literature and art, we have argued, have continually revivified against the grain of "canonical" reception, have now become the sites for the disappearance of meaning and representation.[20] Is, therefore, our recognition of the evil demon of images in the postmodern "age" an acknowledgement, finally, of the contemporary sense of the disappearance – and death – of God: and is there, in addition, grounds for hope in the widest possible sense, artistically, theologically and apocalyptically beyond our present sense of crisis?

Baudrillard's fear is in the perfection of the cinema. Taking films like *Chinatown*, *Barry Lyndon* and *All the President's Men*, he makes of them the point which King David made of Bathsheba: "Your perfection is your greatest flaw."[21] The result is deathly indifference, stimulated only by a fascination for disaster, which is the death of the imagination in a cold, meaningless collage of images.

What has been lost is a living, dialogical relationship between image and imagination, imagination and reference, as the absolutist demon of images transmutes everything, without responsibility or discernment, into Baudrillardian hyperreality. It is this dialogical relationship which counter-readings of the canon of scripture, in literature, art and even the cinema as we have discussed them, sustain, that continues to enliven the traditions of reading and interpretation within communities of belief and religious practice. Every now and then in our age of mechanical reproduction we are disturbed by reminders of this "counter-coherence", reminders of our responsibilities and, uneasily, signs of hope. One hugely popular example of this in the cinema is Eastwood's award-winning film *Unforgiven,* which forms a kind of trilogy with his earlier works *High Plains Drifter* and *Pale Rider*. Still the dark, apocalyptic figure of the avenging angel on a pale horse, Eastwood's William Munny is also a pathetic, almost tragic, broken-down old man – a wretched pig farmer, a wretched father, fearful and deeply loyal to the memory of his wife. The film works simultaneously on the level of the myth of the West, and on the level of the inadequate human beings who both perpetrate the myth and are its victims. We are back with Joseph Heller's King David, a man all-too-human who tragically carries the weight of God's work upon his shoulders.

But the very tragedy of *Unforgiven,* with its ambiguous title, allows space for the reconsideration of its images, a painful dialogue between its two levels which, in the end, calls upon the familiar paradoxes of Christology to grant it the shadow of meaning and justice. We are reminded again, *against the grain,* of the high price to be paid in an economy which overcomes inertia and passive receptivity.

D. H. Lawrence regarded the Book of Revelation as the most influential writing in the whole Bible.[22] A late entry into the canon of the New Testament, "Revelation had to be included in the New Testament, to give the death kiss to the Gospels."[23] Lawrence, like his contemporary C. G. Jung, sees Revelation as inimical to the Christian tradition, a final door closed on the canon, working to its destruction. Lawrence, himself an apocalyptic writer, wrote out of an anger against the vengeful imagery of the chapels of his childhood, turning the "fictions" of Revelation into a vast, deadly myth – a household of demon images. Frank Kermode, in *The Sense of an Ending*, has analysed the process which Lawrence represents:

> Fictions, notably the fiction of apocalypse, turn easily into myths; people will live by that which was designed only to know by. Lawrence would be the writer to discuss here, if there were time; apocalypse works in *Women in Love*, and perhaps even in *Lady Chatterley's Lover*, but not in *Apocalypse*, which is failed myth.[24]

Kermode sharply points out the close association in modernist literature between this mythical sense of apocalypse and the fascist mind (in response to which that herald work of postmodernity, Adorno and Horkheimer's *Dialectic of Enlightenment* (1944), was written), referring in particular to Yeats, Pound, Wyndham Lewis and T. S. Eliot with his anti-Semitism and his "persistent nostalgia for closed, immobile hierarchical societies".[25] Against this modernism, with its chilling relationship to the disastrous history of our century, trapped, as observers of the *post*modern condition have noted, not simply in its own history but in the demonic images which no longer leave room for representation or escape, we now move on to a closer examination of apocalyptic literature in the biblical tradition and in our own time. This and the final chapter will seek to provide some answer to the question "Is there no hope in the evil demon of images?", seeking in the history of the biblical canon, and in the literature and art which it has inspired and continues to inspire in spite of Baudrillardian pessimism and mythic despair.

Notes

1. Jean-François Lyotard, *The Postmodern Condition: A Report on Knowledge*, trans. Geoff Bennington and Brian Massumi (Manchester, 1984) p. xxiii.
2. See Arthur Kroker and David Cook, *The Postmodern Scene: Excremental Culture and Hyper-Aesthetics*, 2nd edn (London, 1991) p. vi.
3. See David E. Klemm, *Hermeneutical Inquiry*, vol. I: *The Interpretation of Texts* (Atlanta, 1986) pp. 22–3.
4. See further below, ch. 9, pp. 123–5.
5. Stephen Sykes, *The Identity of Christianity* (London, 1984) p. 4.
6. Michel Foucault, *The History of Sexuality*, vol. 1, trans. Robert Hurley (Harmondsworth, 1981) pp. 94–5.

7. Jacques Derrida, "Deconstruction and the Other", in Richard Kearney (ed.), *Dialogues with Contemporary Continental Thinkers: The Phenomenological Heritage* (Manchester, 1984) p. 110: Sykes, *Identity of Christianity*, p. 149.
8. Charles E. Winquist, in the Foreword to Robert P. Scharlemann, *Inscriptions and Reflections. Essays in Philosophical Theology* (Charlottesville, 1989) p. viii.
9. See Stanley Fish, "Being Interdisciplinary is So Very Hard to Do", *Profession 89* Modern Language Association of America (1989) 15–22.
10. Seán Hand, Introduction to *The Levinas Reader* (Oxford, 1989) p. 1.
11. John Wild, Introduction to Emmanuel Levinas, *Totality and Infinity: An Essay on Exteriority*, trans. Alphonsus Lingis (The Hague, Boston, London, 1969) p. 13.
12. Andrew Marvell, "On Mr Milton's Paradise Lost". Quoted above, p. 29.
13. See Georges Bataille, *Literature and Evil*, trans. Alastair Hamilton (London, New York, 1985); also Kroker and Cook, *Postmodern Scene*, pp. iff.
14. Julia Kristeva, "Word, Dialogue and Novel", in Toril Moi (ed.), *The Kristeva Reader* (Oxford, 1986) p. 59.
15. Walter Benjamin, "The Work of Art in the Age of Mechanical Reproduction", quoted in Jean Baudrillard, *The Evil Demon of Images*, trans. Paul Patton and Paul Foss (Sydney, 1987) pp. 13–14.
16. Ibid., p. 14.
17. Coppola's film is, of course, based closely upon Joseph Conrad's novella *The Heart of Darkness* (1899).
18. Baudrillard, *Evil Demon of Images*, p. 23.
19. See Richard Harland, *Superstructuralism: The Philosophy of Structuralism and Post-Structuralism* (London, 1987) pp. 181–2.
20. Baudrillard, *Evil Demon of Images*, p. 29.
21. In Torgny Lindgren's *Bathsheba*. See above, ch. 3.
22. See D. H. Lawrence, *Apocalypse* (1931; Harmondsworth, 1974). I am much indebted here to conversations with Christopher Burdon of Glasgow University.
23. Ibid., p. 18.
24. Frank Kermode, *The Sense of an Ending* (Oxford, 1968) pp. 112–14.
25. Ibid., pp. 111–12.

8

Apocalypse Then and Now

That most underrated of biblical scholars, Austin Farrer, begins his study of the Book of Revelation, *A Rebirth of Images*, with these words:

> The human imagination has always been controlled by certain basic images, in which man's own nature, his relation to his fellows, and his dependence upon the divine power find expression . . . in ages for which religion and poetry were a common possession, the basic images lived in the conscious mind . . .[1]

But do we live in an age of either poetry or religion? In what sense do the strong images of Revelation continue to live for us – in the Church's liturgy, in our familiarity with scripture itself – in an age which is haunted by great, demonic images? The Book of Revelation, which has produced such an energetic, often bizarre, yet powerful history of interpretation, has, I contend exploded in our contemporary "apocalyptic" age, itself the literary progenitor of images in literature, screen and culture which do not simply undermine the legitimization of traditional religious structures, but actually run pessimistically counter to the great biblical apocalyptic vision.

We see how our argument is shifting, from the notion of a counter-coherence in the narratives and texts of scripture, to the way in which the scriptural genre of apocalypse may engender images in our postmodern world which, in their bleak pessimism, are far from the triumphant tenor of the concluding book of our canonical scriptures. It may be that this shift is of peculiarly modern date, and that in this most wildly interpreted of biblical texts we now need to recover, like Austin Farrer, a rebirth of images and a renewal of our literary and even, perhaps, theological heritage. In this chapter I want to trace the contrast between apocalypse "then" and "now", and leave the question of recovery and revival to the subsequent chapter, drawing it there into a discussion of this book as a whole.

I sense that our present, deeply pessimistic passion for apocalyptic images and ideas is a recent, twentieth-century phenomenon, a result of the disillusionment after the experiences of world war, totalitarianism, genocide, the nuclear threat, the Cold War. Hans-Georg Gadamer sums up our trauma, and the passing of an age, neatly:

> With World War I a genuine epochal awareness emerged that welded the nineteenth century into a unit of the past. This is true not only in the sense that a bourgeois age, which had united faith in technical progress with the confident expectation of a secured freedom and a civilizing perfectionism, had come to an end. The end is not merely an awareness of leaving an epoch, but above all the *conscious withdrawal* from it, indeed, the sharpest rejection of it.[2]

Gone not only are Enlightenment beliefs in progress, but also from our imaginations, the joys of paradise, which in the nineteenth century remain so touchingly, if often naively, in religious vision. John Martin's canvas *The Plains of Heaven*, a deeply romantic landscape of Revelation 21, was extravagantly praised in the nineteenth century, touring widely with its two companion "Judgement" paintings. Although it now hangs in the Tate Gallery, however, it was sold with its companions in 1935 for a mere £7, a comment, perhaps, on the shift in sensibility. The best description of *The Plains of Heaven* is in Mrs Henry Wood's celebrated novel *East Lynne* (1861), evidence of the picture's popularity and its effect upon a Victorian public:

> "Oh, you should have seen it! There was a river, you know, and boats, beautiful gondolas they looked, taking the redeemed to the shores of Heaven. They were shadowy figures in white robes, myriads and myriads of them, for they reached all up in the air to the holy city; it seemed to be in the clouds, coming down from God. The flowers grew on the banks of the river, pink and blue and violet; all colours, but so bright and beautiful; brighter than our flowers are here."[3]

Few artists have had the courage to envision such a scene. Let John Martin (1789–1854) stand, from his century of faith and doubt, before the traumas of our own time, as a prelude to a brief consideration of apocalyptic literature "then" – in the tradition of the Bible.

The Revelation of St John the Divine has always maintained a strange position in the canon of New Testament literature. Its reception into the canon was slow, although the earliest traditions of the Church generally favour apostolic authorship. About 136 CE, Justin Martyr ascribed it to "John, one of the apostles of Christ" (*Dialogue with Trypho*, lxxxi, 15), as did Tertullian shortly afterwards. Irenaeus (*c*.130–*c*.200 CE) assigned the book's visions specifically to the experience of the persecutions of the closing years of the reign of Domitian (81–96 CE). But by the third century there was widespread doubt concerning the origins of Revelation, and its place in the canon became questionable, dislike of the book surviving into the Reformation among such scholars as Luther and Erasmus. It has been, thus, always a prickly text in the New Testament, its powerful imagery and literary energy much loved and often hated. Linguistically a mess, showing all the signs of an author who thought in one language (Hebrew) and wrote in another (Greek), it nevertheless contains passages of high poetic beauty, and enjoys a literary pedigree which looks back to the Book of Daniel, Enoch and a host of other Jewish apocalypses. Revelation was traditionally conceived of as a prophetic book,[4] in accordance with its opening words, and claims as in 22: 18: "For my part, I give this warning to everyone who is listening to the words of prophecy (τους λόγους τῆς προφητεἰας) in this book." Yet the status of apocalyptic literature as prophecy was always ambiguous: they were related inasmuch as they both claim to be a communication through the Divine Spirit of the character and will and purposes of God, and they both contained an eschatological element, yet they also differ significantly. For, unlike the prophet, the apocalyptic writer despairs of the present time and the goodness of the world as God's world. Second, apocalypse expands its sense of history from the more specific vision of prophecy, and tends towards a determinism, replacing an organic notion of history with a mechanical. Finally, the apocalyptic writers have a harsher vision than the prophets, especially where God's enemies are concerned. As one commentator expresses it (long before Sartre's trilogy *Les Chemins de la liberté* was conceived of), "the iron has entered into their soul".[5]

The violent, stuttering images of Revelation arise not from a fundamental sense of the righteousness of God as much as from a need to solve the difficulties connected with a belief in such righteousness in the face of appalling suffering – a theodical problem which has increasingly haunted our literature and philosophy since Milton and Leibniz, and which has exploded with the stark, inhumane violence of our own century, so peculiarly susceptible in literature, art and cinema to Jean Baudrillard's evil demon of images. The violence which has permeated the pages of the present book is all too real in the origins of Revelation and its use of such words as "slaughtered" ("ἐσφαγμένοι": 6: 9) and "beheaded" ("πεπελεκισμένοι": 20: 4).[6] The violence which, I have argued, lies in our *reading* of scripture – against women, against the "heroes" of salvation history like the tragic King David – in Revelation is explicit. For this reason it inhabits so easily the canon. The "counter-coherence" of literary exposure here resides openly in the text and supplies our own time with images appropriate to its inhumanity, while the comfort of its concluding images of salvation, celebrated in John Martin's picture and in Christian liturgy, is largely forgotten in postmodern apocalypticism.

Yet Jewish apocalyptic in particular, of which Daniel is the best early example, disintegrates the sense of order in both space and time. Its origins were undoubtedly political, for it was a means of comfort in the face of oppression – the alien governments of Hellenic or Roman rulers – and the despair of ever restoring the fortunes of the nation to their former splendour in the Davidic Kingdom. But it was, above all, hopeful, since its predicted chaos was regarded as the prelude to the divine intervention in world affairs, when God would destroy his enemies and establish his kingdom of peace on earth. Thus Rudolf Bultmann summarized New Testament apocalyptic in this way as offering

> a hope which awaits salvation not from a miraculous change in historical (i.e. political and social) conditions, but from a cosmic catastrophe which will do away with all conditions of the present world as it is. The presupposition of this hope is the pessimistic-dualistic view of the Satanic corruption of the total world-complex, which is expressed in the special doctrine of the *two aeons* into which the world's career is divided: the old aeon is approaching its end, and the new aeon will dawn with terror and tribulation. The old world with its periods has an end determined

> by God, and when the day he has determined is here, the judgement of the world will be held by him or by his representative, the Son of Man, who will come on the clouds of heaven; the dead will arise, and men's deeds, good or bad, will receive the reward. But the salvation of the faithful will consist not in national prosperity and splendour, but in the glory of paradise.[7]

There we have it still in our critical reading of scripture – the joy of paradise; Martin's "plains of heaven"; one of Farrer's great images.

But, I suggest, apocalypse "now", still fed by the energy of these images from Revelation, is characterized by a bleak nihilism which has lost all grasp of the great vision of restoration. The nihilism, indeed, permeates the very images themselves, since postmodernity sustains neither the image of the sacred cosmos nor its loss, but only the image that there is no image of the whole of things.[8] The revealing and the cataclysm remain, but nowhere the assurance of peace. And it may be that the realization of this in art and criticism is only now gathering its full momentum. As Robert Detweiler wrote in 1990:

> In his 1972 book, *Where the Wasteland Ends*, Theodore Roszak could refer bleakly to "Environmental collapse, world poverty, technocratic elitism, psychic alienation, the death of the soul" (p. 407), but still posit with some optimism the possibility in our time of "apocatastasis", the actualising of the Gnostic myth of the great restoration (pp. 409–27). This vision nowadays seems merely quaint. With the emergence of the postmodern era (however makeshift and maligned that term may be) has come a deepening, if measured, conviction that these may indeed be the latter days.[9]

No doubt one could argue with this analysis. Nevertheless, if art, literature and film remain significant indicators of our time, it is substantially true I think. And if that is so, my question is, how, if at all, may we recover some sense of the great images of Revelation 21? Or is there merely a showing, merely a cataclysm? Has the violence from which Revelation emerged and which gave it its energy now simply overwhelmed us, the text's birth illuminating these last days, its edginess in the biblical canon now justified?

Jean Baudrillard, as was intimated in the previous chapter, offers us one of the bleakest of postmodern apocalyptic visions. The very style of his writing bears some resemblance to the great tradition of apocalyptic writings, being hyperbolic and declarative, often unsystematic and totalizing, shattering and radical. Baudrillard's 1981 work *Simulacra and Simulations* breaks down any possible control by the codes and conventions which govern our societies. From "reality", he argues, we move into a hyperreality in which a simulation is different from a fiction or a lie in that it not only presents an absence as a presence, the imaginary as real, but it also undermines any contrast it may have with the real, absorbing the real within itself. We live now in a world only of self-referential signs in which there is no order except the violent order of disorder, in which is unveiled "structures of domination when no one is dominating, nothing is being dominated and no ground exists for a principle of liberation from domination".[10] In such a world there is no distinction between death and life, and no power is tolerable inasmuch as only the intolerable exists. In such a postmodern world, Baudrillard would say, the only possibility for us is to press on to a position of unsustainable excess, a pure nihilism. The only escape is through the final cataclysm. His gospel of freedom runs thus:

> a system is abolished only by pushing it into hyperlogic, by forcing it into an excessive practice which is equivalent to a brutal amortization. "You want us to consume – O.K., let's consume always more, and anything whatsoever; for any useless and absurd purpose."[11]

Such systematic abandonment of system abandons even the presumption that anything has meaning or use-value, the image simply that there is no image. But in Baudrillard's postmodern nightmare there is nothing more positive in view after the violation of the status quo and the violence of self-destruction.

In response to such bleakness, however, one might suggest, after Frank Kermode, and in complete opposition to Lyotard (see above p. 96), that *crisis* is a way of thinking about "the moment", and is not inherent in the moment itself. Without returning to a myth of restoration, we should address the reason why film, art and literature continue creatively to present us with apocalyptic fictions which reflect upon the breakdown of our civilization – ways of thinking about a situation in which, as Baudrillard admits, we have lost touch with "reality". In what sense, then, is his nightmare "real", the end simulated as a warning against its own fulfilment, an invitation to us, it may even be, to recognize afresh a radical theological revision of vision?

The cinema has, understandably, employed the strong images of apocalypse, sometimes in a disturbing intertextuality with the biblical text, perhaps most notably in recent years in Adrian Lyne's deeply moving film *Jacob's Ladder* (1990). Ingmar Bergman's classic *The Seventh Seal* (1957)[12] captures the pictorial strength which masks an almost deconstructed narrative that characterizes the atmosphere of Revelation's images. But I want to pause for one moment on a far more popular, mainstream Hollywood film which in many ways is extremely crude, though technically brilliant. James Cameron's *Terminator II: Judgment Day* (1991), partly because of its popular appeal, manages to capture a feeling for apocalypse which can easily be lost in the careful, anxious interpretations of critical or liturgical reading. This is a film about a world at war, people faced with ultimate destruction, heroism against the odds and in the midst of chaos. It is a world, in other words, not altogether unlike that of the Church under the Domitian persecutions, when a tiny community held out for truth against the odds and needed the spirit of apocalyptic to survive. It is, however, a film which has failed to grasp the deep pessimism of its own culture, as perceived by Baudrillard and others, and ultimately does not appreciate the dark demons of its own images with their totalitarian implications. One of the most frightening aspects of *Terminator II* is its almost wilful lack of self-perception in a violent world.

The film certainly has very many of the hallmarks of early apocalyptic – the violence, breakdown of order, and (paradoxically most disturbing for me because here sentimental) a vision of restoration. As so often in apocalypse, the film pursues its "narrative" by a radical reordering of temporal sequence. A machine from the future returns to the present to try and prevent its own time from taking place. "Judgment Day" is always both future and present, something that will happen and something that is happening now.[13] The tradition of apocalyptic writing, coming after prophetic literature, precisely recognizes that it must act as a warning against its own fulfilment – that judgement is both in the present, when the chaos which we may not even be wholly aware of, actually *is* the chaos that we all fear. Even as we wait and dread it, it is in our midst: judgement day is now, and yet perhaps it can be avoided even so.

This dark and violent product of the Hollywood film industry is, in fact, firmly within the tradition of the great biblical epics of Cecil B. De Mille, John Huston and others, which we considered in Chapter 6. Actually a reflection on how America would see itself – heroic, salvific, defender of the truth – it leaves the canonical text of scripture largely undisturbed, and finally *unread* in the context of contemporary tragedy, modern violence (against women, or minority groups, for example), or postmodernity. Ultimately it sustains the apocalyptic vision of John Martin's great paintings, with all their finally naive and sentimental faith. And yet there are moments in the film of appalling, unsustainable violence which *we*, in our Baudrillardian world, have never resolved – not having our Arnold Swarzeneggers on hand. Particularly terrifying is the central dream sequence which portrays ordinary family life in a great city – children playing in the park, young mothers – devastated by a vast nuclear explosion. It is a complex moment in the film. As we watch we dread it because we know exactly what it is, for it has already happened in our history in the cities of Hiroshima and Nagasaki. And yet it remains, at the same time, unthinkable and unimaginable – the incursion of utter chaos (for which we must bear some responsibility) into our domestic lives.

What makes apocalyptic so unnerving – and it happens in *Terminator II* – is that it portrays a reality which we recognize as our own, yet is beyond our imagining. The reintroduction of interest in the language and images of Revelation at particular moments in history – the Romantics after the French Revolution, postmodern criticism, art and literature in our own time – reflects an experience of violent upheaval, as in the early persecutions of Christians, and a recognition that what we experience *is* unthinkable, which somehow must be articulated as a prelude to salvation. In *Terminator II*, against the odds, there is survival, even though at the cost of the hero's own "life". What bothers me, however, is that so much of our postmodern literature, perhaps with more honesty and less kitsch than the Hollywood epic (who knows?), takes up the language of apocalypse, but without any sense of rebirth or restoration: what, now, of a rebirth of images such as have sustained our eschatological belief and hopes?

Contemporary fiction, I believe, does offer us texts which envision Baudrillard's hyperreality, with a poetics which are something akin to the Book of Revelation yet without comfort. The British novelist J. G. Ballard was born in Shanghai, China, in 1930. His fictions are saturated in biblical and religious language and imagery, in particular the language and images of apocalyptic, and perhaps most disturbingly in his most postmodern work to date, *The Atrocity Exhibition* (1969). In this fiction, Ballard makes no attempt to write in the mode of literary realism. The book is a series of sequences devoid of narrative coherence, a text of profound violent incoherence of which one can perhaps best say that it is within the event of the mental breakdown of its central consciousness who / which is either patient or doctor in a kaleidoscope of shifting identities (Travis, Talbot, Trabert, Talbert, etc.).

The first word of *The Atrocity Exhibition* is "apocalypse", its setting an annual exhibition of art in a mental institution "with the theme of world cataclysm". Reality and unreality merge in simulated intercourse: familiar images of the American consumer society of the 1960s clash meaninglessly in a chaos of sexuality, car crash, napalm and presidential assassination. Without plot the images become wildly and violently repetitious, deathridden and challenging of any attempt to impose meaning upon them, reduced to voyeurism and mere bodily stimulation. Here is a typical example from a chapter entitled "Tolerance of the Human Face":

> *Sequence in slow-motion: a landscape of highways and embankments, evening light of fading concrete, intercut with images of a young woman's body. She lay on her back, her wounded face stressed like fractured ice. With almost dream-like calm, the camera explored her bruised mouth, the thighs dressed in a dark lacework of blood. The quickening geometry of her body, its terraces of pain and sexuality, became a source of intense excitement. Watching from the embankment, Travers found himself thinking of the eager deaths of his childhood.*[14]

The American dream gone sour – and yet we have seen its decrepitude beneath the dazzle of its burnished surface. Apocalypse – a revelation – an exhibition of the atrocities which we mask with our systems of reality: a narrative fractured by the weight of its own powerful images disintegrating its linearity: just as in Book of Revelation, chapter 17, John of Patmos is shown the Whore of Babylon and "In her hand she held a gold cup, full of obscenities and the foulness of her fornication. . . ."

To have seen is to have felt the discomfort of the violation of the violence of system, and yet in the very fragmentation of familiar images, new intersections may furtively take place within the written word in a rebirth of images. In *The Atrocity Exhibition*, as in Dostoevsky's *Notes from the Underground* (1864), "where these planes intersect, images are born, some kind of valid reality begins to clarify itself".[15] Thus one critic of Ballard argues, though I find it hard to perceive in *The Atrocity Exhibition* any validity beyond utter perversity and chaos denying all reason and all faith.

As has always been the case, modern (and postmodern) apocalypses are disturbingly anchored in contemporary political agendas, worried by both the necessity and irrelevance of history. From Patmos to Warsaw is not such a long way, as we find Konwicki – author, hero and narrator of the novel *A Minor Apocalypse* (1979) – recognizing a revelation as he steps closer to his martyrdom in communist Warsaw. Since Revelation, apocalypse has always been an "exhortation to martyrdom",[16] an act, maybe, of ultimate faith or utter futility. An ironic revelation this is, it is true, on Konwicki's last day, at the end of the world. But, perhaps it is the irony which we have missed – that the "God of Mercy" *whom we have created in toil, pain and agony* must suffer the apocalypse of his own death in an act of the deepest and purest iconoclasm. Maybe here we can begin to feel in our deepest pessimisms towards a rebirth of images, and a revivifying of the tradition of apocalypse.

In Tadeusz Konwicki's fictional celebration, the voyage into nothingness echoes with a note of responsibility which belies Baudrillardian nihilism in the resurrection of nothingness. That note sounds repeatedly in postmodern fiction in a secretive rediscovery of the insistent life of these images through the patient agonies of communist Poland: in the apocalypse of race and gender which, in Toni Morrison's *Beloved* explodes the moment of knowing by a black woman into a startling encounter with "otherness" beyond gender and beyond race – a story to be told but not passed on.[17] It is sounded in the political feminism of Michele Roberts's *The Wild Girl* in dreams which re-politicize the visions of John of Patmos, for the Whore of men's deepest nightmares (and secret passions) becomes also the raped victims by whom they stand judged.

Apocalyptic writings continually invert, continually enact a crisis of discontinuity. Careless of our carefully constructed, guarding principles of mimesis, they violently unhinge the correlation between the images of our world and their reference. Yet perhaps the real violence lies in the correlation and not in its violation. Thus, inescapably political – as in Mark 13, as in Revelation – apocalypse is attracted to the ideological sufferings, the radical divisions and the sexual oppressions of our contemporary world. In Ballard, as in so many writers, the nuclear holocaust is perhaps the dominant apocalyptic "image" in our present simulations of the end: it is either, in the words of the *Bhagavad Gita*, the "splendour of the Mighty One" or "Death, the shatterer of worlds".[18] An image which haunts our fiction and our screens, the mushroom cloud is matched only perhaps, by the genocidal images of Auschwitz and Belsen. Primo Levi, a Jewish survivor of the camps and eventual suicide, wrote in one of his short stories:

> "As long as God continues to sin with Lilith, there will be blood and trouble on Earth. But one day a powerful being will come – the one we are all waiting for. He will make Lilith die and put an end to God's lechery, and to our exile."[19]

Lilith, hag and succuba of ancient myth, is mentioned only once in the Old Testament, in Isaiah 34: 14, as a female demon associated with night and storm. Whence this new Messianic enormity, then? It stems from the Holocaust survivor – Levi, Emmanuel Levinas, Paul Celan – who recognizes in this apocalypse (which silences all our theological excuses) that here *all* are "responsible" who survive, without even having decided to be so and prior to any voluntary act. There is no escape, even for us as readers, and even for God.[20] Thus, in his essay "To Love the Torah More than God",[21] Emmanuel Levinas, rabbinically expresses his belief in the absent God, his face obscured in the fire of the ovens, the Whore of Babylon who has been raped, who reads the charge and pleads for both the prosecution and the defence: an apocalypse without sentimental communion (Levinas's words, not mine) as "Protection against the madness of direct contact with the Sacred".

Another Jewish survivor – though like Primo Levi, a suicide – Walter Benjamin regarded as his most treasured possession the painting by Paul Klee entitled *Angelus Novus*. Benjamin's description of the picture has become justly famous:

> A Klee painting named "Angelus Novus" shows an angel looking as though he is about to move away from something he is fixedly contemplating. His eyes are staring, his mouth is open, his wings are spread. This is how one pictures the angel of history.

> His face is turned towards the past. Where we perceive a chain of events, he sees one single catastrophe which keeps piling wreckage upon wreckage and hurls it in front of his feet. The angel would like to stay, awaken the dead, and make whole what is smashed. But a storm is blowing from Paradise; it has got caught in his wings with such violence that the angel can no longer close them. The storm irresistibly propels him into the future to which his back is turned, while the pile of debris before him grows skyward. The storm is what we call progress.[22]

This thesis on the philosophy of history presents a tragic perspective on the salvation history read in the Bible in the ternary cosmology of creation, fall and re-creation. As Adam and Eve are expelled from Paradise, deterred from re-entry by the guard with whirling and flashing sword, the narrative from Genesis 4 becomes not one of gradual restoration, but rather a tragic backing into the future, history blown along by the anger of the divine storm. With wandering steps and slow we stumble upon our march of progress, too easily persuading ourselves in our theological anxiety to justify the voice of God in the canonical paradigm,[23] that the tragedy and exclusions of human experience in the narratives and images of scripture do not take place.

Both Baudrillard and Ballard know the tragic *Angelus Novus* – one who would save us, but who is himself driven back from Paradise amidst the wreckage of history. Blind to the future, he looks longingly back upon the catastrophe which has already happened, and we configure it as our history, expecting the tragedy that is yet to be.

The nihilism of the postmodern apocalypse, it may be, intimates a rebirth of images which only those who have been utterly consumed by it could begin to utter – Primo Levi, Paul Celan, Walter Benjamin all committed suicide, realizing that only death was now possible, literature always and already (as Roland Barthes knew) a posthumous affair.

The violence of apocalypse exposes, reveals and exhibits these simulacra of freedom and justice which, we suppose, give order to our temporal existence. No Hollywood-created myth can restore this destruction. Too often we resist its message in our addiction to our well-ordered atrocities, but in the literature and literality of the apocalypse there may be a proper demand for that "hypermorality" and "hyperreality" that is an acute and often painful awareness of the radical evil which resides at the heart of the human condition and its systems of control. The unbearable catastrophes which we now have glimpsed in our time are pressing and necessary for us to recognize and see if we are to survive at all, for they effect a clarification and an unbearable, unthinkable and finally unreable revelation: that the modern, and postmodern, nihilism embedded in contemporary literature and critical thought is also a modern apocalypticism, most obviously present in Nietzsche and inaugurated by William Blake. It has been described by Thomas Altizer as "a new creation, and an absolutely new creation, but a new creation that can only be a consequence of the final ending of an old totality",[24] and, in Altizer's perception, a death of God.

Such a vision can cost us nothing less than everything, and finally the recognition of the death of the greatest of all images, God himself, in the purest of iconoclasms – an act so deep that it can, perhaps we may dare to say, only be of God himself: pure apocalypse is revealed as an absolute reversal of the Godhead "which must necessarily and finally end every potency or echo of a once and for all and irreversible beginning".[25] Only then may the "Angelus Novus" be freed from his tragic struggle as the storm from Paradise loses its power and its obsessional influence over our theologizing and attempts to justify the ways of God in the pages of scripture. The sacred has always been an arena for violence and the monstrous in a call for sacrifice – above all, for the Christian tradition, the sacrifice within the Godhead of the Son at the moment when Christ the divine expresses his own foresakenness by God: God most Godlike in his utter abandonment by God; God the wholly other, other even than itself. Here is the full unveiling of the atrocity exhibition which is our history, an absolutism only of distrust, a dilapidation beyond all our decisive, violent decisions for the truth.[26]

Perhaps here alone, in such a dislocation and deadly rebirth of sacred images, is a justification of that incident in the Book of Judges, so resolutely avoided by most biblical commentators, in which a woman is repeatedly raped, slaughtered and cut into twelve pieces, one for each of the tribes of the Chosen People of God. Or if justification is an inappropriate word, it is at least a shocking us into vision.

Revelation 21 celebrates the vision of the New Jerusalem. From the first chapter it is clear that the book is intended to be read in church, its text inviolate available for neither additions nor subtractions (22: 18–19), as both a warning, an explanation and a comfort. What I have argued through contemporary art, film and literature, is that the keynote of the apocalypse is a violent one – it is a literature born from the experience of violence in persecution, and the sense of chaos which forms the necessary prelude to "the end". As Herder recognized, Revelation is, in the first instance, a poem rather than a philosophical or historical treatise. I suggest, therefore, that poetry and art will most immediately reverberate with its symbols, images and recapitulative structure. Written, perhaps, for liturgical use, or at least for reading within the Christian community, the apocalypse nevertheless is awakened in times like our own, which again have experienced violence, persecution, and a great, looming sense of an immanent ending and disintegration.

Postmodernity, therefore, is itself deeply apocalyptic, though it has so far betrayed few insights into "apocatastasis" – the myth of the great restoration. What it *may* be struggling towards, however, is a radical, Christological recovery in its deeply painful and passionate meditations on suffering, sacrifice and finality: meditations, as Thomas Altizer might say, as the *wholly* new in the abandonment of the old totality – nothing less than a death of God. Speaking of such unspeakability, the fictions of Ballard, Morrison, Konwicki and others may indeed be returning us to a scriptural, apocalyptic vision which the configurations of our history and the systematic readings of our theology and its hermeneutics have served to blot out.

We are being given a terrible and terrific choice.[27] A powerful element in apocalyptic literature has always been the final judgement. In the exhibition of atrocities, the choice is now stark – the unthinkable can be thought in a rebirth of images, or else thought becomes unthinkable, and there is only a deathly silence.

The extraordinary technology of Hollywood achieved in *Terminator II* is simply another version of the Hollywood epic, with its celebration of the values claimed by the USA itself as the land of freedom – another version of the myth of the paradisal New World. But it is in the darker, bleaker visions of the art of post-Holocaust literature, or the post-nuclear fictional nightmares of Ballard or Russell Hoban, that a more substantial re-reading of apocalyptic literature may be taking place, against the grain of our religious and theological training beginning to effect, most painfully, a rebirth of images from the chaos.

Such will be the starting point of the next chapter.

Notes

1. Austin Farrer, *A Rebirth of Images: The Making of St John's Apocalypse* (Westminster, 1949) p. 13.
2. Hans-Georg Gadamer, "The Philosophical Foundations of the Twentieth Century", in *Philosophical Hermeneutics*, trans. and ed. David E. Linge (Berkeley and Los Angeles, 1976) pp. 107–29.
3. Quoted in Bruce Bernard, *The Bible and its Painters* (London, 1988) p. 299.
4. See, further, Bernard McGinn, "Revelation", in Robert Alter and Frank Kermode (eds), *The Literary Guide to the Bible* (London, 1987) pp. 523–41.
5. James Hastings (ed.), *A Dictionary of the Bible*, vol. 1 (Edinburgh, 1898) p. 110.
6. See, further, C. F. D. Moule, *The Birth of the New Testament*, 2nd edn (London, 1966) pp. 115–17.
7. Rudolf Bultmann, *Theology of the New Testament*, vol. 1, trans. K. Grobel (London, 1965) pp. 4–5.
8. See David E. Klemm, Introduction to *Hermeneutical Inquiry*, vol. 1: *The Interpretation of Texts* (Atlanta, 1986) pp. 19–24.
9. Robert Detweiler, "Apocalyptic Fiction and the End(s) of Realism", in David Jasper and Colin Crowder (eds), *European Literature and Theology in the Twentieth Century: Ends of Time* (London, 1990) p. 154.
10. Jean Baudrillard, *Simulacra and Simulations*, trans. Paul Foss, Paul Patton and Philip Beitchman (New York, 1983) p. 154.
11. Jean Baudrillard, *In the Shadow of the Silent Majorities*, trans. Paul Foss, Paul Patton and John Johnston (New York, 1983) p. 46. See also Richard Harland, *Superstructuralism: The Philosophy of Structuralism and Post-Structuralism* (London and New York, 1987) pp. 176–83.
12. For a good discussion of religion in Bergman's films, see D. Z. Phillips, *Through a Darkening Glass: Philosophy, Literature and Cultural Change* (Oxford, 1982) ch. 9: "Ingmar Bergman's Reductionism", pp. 133–64.
13. Another example of this in modern literature is in Kurt Vonnegut's *Slaughterhouse 5* (1970). The inhabitants of the planet Tralfamadore know that the universe will end when a test pilot experiments with new fuels for their flying saucers. The moment is always future, and always present: "He has *always* pressed it, and he always *will*. We *always* let him and we always *will* let him. The moment is *structured* that way" (Vintage edition, 1991) p. 84.
14. J. G. Ballard, *The Atrocity Exhibition* (1970; London, 1979) p. 73.
15. See William G. Doty, "Exhibiting the Grammar of Apocalypse: Ballard's *The Atrocity Exhibition*", *Art Papers*, vol. 15, no. 6 (1991) 36.
16. See Moule, *Birth of the New Testament*, p. 115.
17. Toni Morrison, *Beloved* (London, 1988) pp. 274–5.
18. These images from the *Bhagavad-Gita* pervade Robert Jungk's chilling history of the discovery and development of the atomic bomb, *Brighter Than a Thousand Suns* (1956).
19. Primo Levi, *Moments of Reprieve*, trans. Ruth Feldman (London, 1987) p. 44.

20. See Susan Handelman, *Fragments of Redemption* (Bloomington, 1991) p. 212: and *The Slayers of Moses* (Albany, 1982) pp. 171–2.
21. E. Levinas, *Difficile liberté: Essai sur le Judaisme*, in *Presences du Judaisme* (Paris, 1963).
22. Walter Benjamin, *Illuminations*, ed. Hannah Arendt, trans. Harry Zohn (1955; Fontana, 1992) p. 249.
23. See James A. Sanders, *Canon and Community* (Philadelphia, 1984) p. 68.
24. Thomas J. J. Altizer, *Genesis and Apocalypse* (Louisville, 1990) p. 22.
25. Ibid., p. 184.
26. See René Girard, *Violence and the Sacred*, trans. Patrick Gregory (Baltimore and London, 1977).
27. I adapt this phrase from the remarkable, final short story written by John Cowper Powys, "Cataclysm" (published 1985).

9

A Rebirth of Images

This chapter of my study will take the form of a kind of dialogue with a book which deserves wider recognition than it has, I think, received; that is, John Barton's Bampton Lectures for 1988, *People of the Book? The Authority of the Bible in Christianity* (1988). Professor Barton is a pupil of Austin Farrer, who worked in an Oxford which was philosophically and critically antagonistic to him and almost certainly incapable of understanding what he was saying about the Bible.

Essential to Farrer's reading of scripture, as Barton recognizes,[1] is his realization that any doctrine of the Bible belongs to the epistemological portion of Christian theology. That is, our approach to the canon of scripture has to do in the first instance with our *knowledge* of God, and such knowledge emerges out of an interaction between the reader of the text and certain irreducible images. Thus far I can cautiously travel with Farrer, but with increasing unease. For the nature of these images seems to me to be more problematic than either Farrer or Barton recognize, being both constructive of religious commitment and at the same time deconstructive of that faith which too quickly tends to solidify the canonical authority of the Bible.

Both John Barton and Austin Farrer are Church of England clergymen, saturated with the spirit of the Thirty-Nine Articles of Religion, of which Article 6 declares that "Holy Scripture containeth all things necessary to salvation", listing "the names and number of the canonical books". For them, ecclesiastical authority defines a closed and fixed list of books which constitute the *maximum* set or writings which can be appealed to as defining the Christian faith.[2] Thus, even though Barton throughout his book fully recognizes the distinction between revelation and the human words of the books of the Bible, nevertheless his criticisms of the notion of canon leave essentially intact the authority of texts as guardians of those images which "contain all things necessary to salvation". That is, he fails to acknowledge the counter-coherence in the text which both recognizes the demonic power of images as destructive yet, at the same time, necessarily and profitably *deconstructive* of dangerous expectations of consistency inherent in the notion of canon. From the word made flesh, the tendency is rather to the flesh made word in an overdependence on the semantic stability of the authoritative text.

I do not deny Professor Barton's repeated recognition of the "semantic indeterminacy"[3] of sacred tests, though this indeterminacy, in this instance, is a hermeneutic means of preserving, through the awkwardnesses and vagaries of textuality, the *stability* of the truths which lie protected beneath the shield of the canon. As is so often the case in the exercise of biblical criticism, Barton prefers to shine the light of his insight *through* the text to that which lies beyond it, explicitly emphasizing "how essential it is to see the Bible as a Text which we can get behind".[4] In the end such self-confessed "excavative work" – an activity we have repeatedly been warned against by Robert Alter[5] – simply disrupts and fragments the text and finally distracts us from the necessary task of encountering it in its aporetic, disturbing immediacy. Both Barton and Farrer, for whose work, as must be clear by now, I have the highest regard, nevertheless trouble me because their initial assumptions are *religious* and *theological*. In their primary move away from scripture, which is a wholly commendable evasion of that "bibliolatry" which plagues the Christian tradition, they shift instead to the community of faith which, in a classic hermeneutic circle, imposes upon scripture that tradition of reading which claims its authority from its pages. In canonical criticism, this is not much different from the assumptions of James Sanders (see above, Chapter 2).

What instead I have been proposing is a literary turn following, at once, S. T. Coleridge's requirement for reading in *Biographia Literaria* (1817) of a "willing suspension of disbelief", and also at the same time a willing suspension of *belief*. That is, we must accept a situation of marginality in our reading of the Bible, living on the border that both joins and separates belief and unbelief.[6] We may then move *towards* the assumption with which Farrer and Barton begin, granting its religious and theological claims thereby a greater authenticity and a greater freedom. Far from being members of that great secularized culture from which Pascal expressed his amazement in the *Pensées* "that people do not fall into despair over such a wretched state", we continue to live in hope, accepting uncertainty and lack of definition precisely as freedoms to be celebrated.

The "Address to the Reader" which prefaces the Authorized (King James) Version of the Bible (1611) describes Scripture as

> a tree, or rather a whole paradise of trees of life, which brings forth fruits every month, and the fruit thereof is for meat, and the leaves for medicine. It is not a pot of manna or a cruse of oil, which were for memory only, or for a meal's meat or two, but as it were a shower of heavenly bread sufficient for a whole host, be it never so great, and as it were a whole cellarful of oil vessels; whereby all our necessities may be provided for, and our debts discharged. In a word it is a pantry of wholesome food against mouldy traditions; a pharmacist's shop (Saint Basil calleth it) of preservatives against poisoned heresies; a code of profitable laws against rebellious spirits; a treasury of most costly jewels against beggarly rudiments. Finally, a fountain of most pure water springing up into everlasting life.[7]

The passage is, of course, not only deeply theological, it is permeated with biblical imagery. But I offer it again here, because it also effects a remarkable literary release from the constraining context of traditional reading and appropriation. It, so to speak, returns the reader to the lost paradise of images before those images became an (often nostalgic) part of a theological and religious tradition of salvation history, a tradition absorbed in human waywardness and deviation. This literary "paradise" may present a hermeneutic possibility to the ever self-reflexive, mouldy traditions of theological reading within the communities of faith, an irreducible and poetic return to a rebirth of images in a new appropriation of the Bible. Perhaps this is why the King James Version has remained so powerful in our English reception of the Bible, a "classic" in the full sense of the word.

This is not, of course, a static notion – fountains are living and continually changing, or otherwise they would cease to be fountains. But the question remains, how do we identify these healthful images, shedding the misdealing and dangerous mould of traditions, restoring them to wholeness of life? Even more, how do we distinguish them from the demonic images which were the subject of our reflection in Chapter 7? Here I return again to John Barton. The problem lies, it seems to me, in his specific concern to distinguish between the "classic" text, and the "sacred" text in the canon of scripture. "Sacred texts", he asserts, "tend to be semantically indeterminate, for they have to be read as supporting the religious system to which they belong, even at the expense of their natural sense."[8] Now, of course, Professor Barton is quick to defend the power of the Biblical text against such a determined fate. Nevertheless, the thrust of his argument within the traditions of believing does tend to confirm and affirm this definition of the sacred text, even as he denies it. Determination emerges from the "religious system" which confirms the authority of the text within the canonical tradition. But, I would argue, it is precisely the *semantic* determination which emerges not from the system but from the text itself – its narratives, poetics and images. "Read the Bible like any other book, and only then will its authoritative status become apparent" – the nineteenth-century insight remains pertinent.

We should not, therefore, be moving behind the text, nor tolerating semantic indeterminacy in support of a religious system, but responding to the encounter with the text as we engage with it dialogically. For, as Barton rightly points out, it is encounter, and neither information nor opinion, which is mediated by the biblical text.[9] What is required of the reader in such textual encounter is, first, discernment and, second, that commitment referred to in my Preface, in the context of Ian Ramsey's work. That is, reading becomes a celebratory act of worship, a restoration of ethical vision, perceived and confirmed in its reconstruction of intersubjective relationships and its establishment of value across the space of the text.

How have we exorcised the demon of images which began to haunt us two chapters ago? There, as Walter Benjamin suggested, we found that an image is most diabolical when it appears most in conformity to reality. Such conformity itself is diabolical, and the "postmodern" voice is, perhaps, a lament over an age which narcissistically merely sees its own face reflected in all things and in the frenzy of consumerism which rushes to its own destruction without difference and without originality.

The religious traditions which have been sustained by a conformity to the "canonical authority" of the Bible, as they perceive it, are always in danger of this most diabolical perversity. Dostoevsky was profoundly aware of this, as was Kierkegaard. What this book has tried to suggest is that the canon of scripture has always sustained its authority precisely *because* it both invites readings within the traditions of worship and criticism, and at the same time counter-readings, so often expressed in art, poetry and literature, which enliven, problematize, offer hope *in spite of* themselves. They offer an invitation to be bold, radical, taking leaps of faith into new stories so that the old may still have life. As Rebecca Adams, an editor of the journal *Religion and Literature,* has recently well expressed it in an editorial in an issue entitled "Violence, Difference, Sacrifice":

> to accept death voluntarily, and to accept it as fully human, transforms the narrative one is in. By contemplating the death of God . . . we too may choose to place ourselves in this larger nonviolent story – an act that might be understood as the imitation of Christ, stepping into Christ's place in relation to death and life. Only by entering a new myth of this type, I suggest, can we escape the cultural myth of sacrifice and the victimage it entails. The death of God . . . can be thought of as a koan which forms the basis of a new metanarrative, a new ethical and religious aesthetic based on openness to death, and thus to life.[10]

Escaping the cultural myth is to re-fictionalize, that is to preserve the narrative tension which guarantees the life of moral responsibility, receptivity and the decision to give and accept love. In a further illustration, I return to Rembrandt's art of the Bible to indicate what I mean – how the images of art play upon the biblical story in a final celebration which both confirms and overcomes the traditions of reading and interpretation within the communities of faith: the canon confirmed and infinitely expanded.

In the British Museum there is a small pen and ink drawing by Rembrandt depicting the Prodigal Son of Luke 16 as a swineherd: "so he went and attached himself to one of the local landowners, who sent him onto his farm to mind the pigs. He would have been glad to fill his belly with the pods that the pigs were eating; and no one gave him anything" (vv. 15–16). It is probable that Rembrandt was looking back to Dürer's celebrated engraving of the same moment of repentance, but while Dürer presents a full scene, replete with all sorts of buildings, Rembrandt has stripped his drawing back to the bare essentials: the kneeling boy, the feeding pigs and the merest hint of a structure. Rubens also painted the scene, slightly earlier than Rembrandt's little picture, with a busy, thriving farmyard which throws into greater relief the boy's utter destitution. Rubens has also added to the Bible narrative by introducing the figure of a buxom farmer's wife looking with pity on the lad while she actually feeds the pigs. And there may be more to her look than innocent concern, for behind a pillar of the barn lurks a very angry-looking and clearly jealous farmer! Even as a ragged down-and-out the playboy obviously has his charms.

But what of Rembrandt's rough sketch? It is more touching than any other I have seen, the emaciated figure of the Prodigal kneeling among the feeding pigs, his arms leaning on a stick, his gaze directed forward in inward intensity. This is precisely the moment when he "comes to his senses" (v. 17), literally "he came into himself", as though the self had been absent from itself and now returns to itself. Although his gaze is inward – that unseeing, all-seeing look of so many of Rembrandt's great figures – he significantly now looks forward. In a great, and much earlier Rembrandt painting[11] of the Prodigal Son squandering his wealth, as a rich young man in a tavern, with glass in hand and girl on knee, he is looking over his shoulder. Here his body is turned away from us, but his face, with its vacuous grin, looks behind him and towards the viewer. (Rembrandt, it should be recalled, used himself as a model for this young wastrel, the woman on his knee a portrait of his wife Saskia.)

In the movement from the rake to the repentant swineherd, the Prodigal has turned his head to face forward, returning to himself to look sorrowfully, ecstatically, on his life, but at least now with a movement towards the future. The experience is literally, in the turning of the head, one of *metanoia,* a turning around and a reordering of mind and life. It is the experience described by Augustine in Book VIII of the *Confessions* when he describes the Lord as "turning me around to look at myself. For I had placed myself behind my own back, refusing to see myself. You were setting me before my own eyes so that I could see how sordid I was. . . ."[12] So Rembrandt's Prodigal turns his head and sees *himself,* before himself.

I am reminded here, too, of Martin Luther in his commentary on the Epistle to the Galatians, when he speaks of faith as placing us outside ourselves (*"fides ponit nos extra nos"*) – the repentant sinner one who literally faces him or herself, stands outside the self in order to return to the self once again. Hence we might even speak of the ecstasy of the Prodigal's inward gaze. It is this moment when one perceives one's being "as not" – one's true self as wholly other than that by which one has hitherto defined oneself and has been defined. To the elder brothers of this world the Prodigal remains the prodigal, that which he *has* been, moral judgement continuing to cloud the radicality of the parable's re-vision. Repeatedly the stories of Jesus go out of their way to avoid the intrusion of morality, for their metaphorical concern operates at a far more radical level of reversal. Their radically new vision of the world grants absolutely no information until after one has entered into it and experienced it from inside itself.

A painful, visionary moment of leaving the self in order to come to the self. Often our first reaction will be to refuse to enter such a vision of the world and we seek to translate it into the comfortable normality of our ordinary linguistic world. Herbert Marcuse once expressed very clearly this problem for poetry:

> The poet [he said] might answer that indeed he wants his poetry to be understandable and understood (that is why he writes it), but if what he says could be said in terms of ordinary language he would probably have done so in the first place. He might say: Understanding of my poetry presupposes the collapse and invalidation of precisely that universe of discourse and behaviour into which you want to translate it.

The intense gaze of Rembrandt's Prodigal Son indicates his painful, risky entrance into a new universe of discourse. Immediately, in the parable, he speaks *to himself*, to the self whom, for the first time, he faces. And his world becomes a risky place.

Let Rembrandt pick up the story again. There is the great and justly famous painting of the return of the Prodigal Son[13] in which the boy kneels before his loving father, his head resting on the father's breast, one of his sandals lost in the haste which has brought the two together. Now we do not see the boy's gaze, as his face is buried in the old man's coat, but the inwardness of his repentant look is now reciprocated by the lost inward gaze of the father, looking *at* nothing, but wrapped within a whole world inhabited only by these two, and inaccessible to the other three figures present in the picture who remain silently at a distance. The son is lost and wholly found in the father; losing himself he has come to himself. Often commented on are the two hands of the father resting on the lad's shoulders protectively: the left a powerful man's hand, the right (perhaps the hand of God, the *dextra dei*?) beautifully slender, the hand of a gentle woman. He is to the boy all things – both father and mother. Cynics remark here on Rembrandt's relative clumsiness in painting hands. Well, I do not see much evidence of that elsewhere in his work. And the picture, like the parable of Luke's Gospel, is what it is.

But I would draw your attention further to a second, also very late, picture of this moment in the story by Rembrandt, another small pen and brush drawing, which captures the world of the parable beautifully even as it deviates from the letter of it.[14] Almost devoid of background apart from the figures of the father and the son, this drawing has one further rather strange figure, a small boy who looks on in surprise at the moment of reunion. The sense here is of the violent collision between the two central figures, the father's discarded stick lying on the ground behind him, the kneeling son almost lurching forward as the old man's right hand supports him, his left hand resting on his head. Once again, they exist in a total, inaccessible world of their own in which that which was lost is wholly found: a world violently and eagerly rediscovered and embraced.

It all turns upon that moment among the pigs when the Prodigal Son comes to himself, and a new world is created. Tradition and criticism have, apparently from the earliest days, tended to translate the New Testament parables into comfortable moral normalcy, making *examples* of their radical re-visioning. I have turned to Rembrandt because meditation on his paintings and drawings of Luke 15 are not weighted with pedantic concerns for *ipsissima verba,* but respect, Rembrandt being a great artist (and not one who is closely concerned with a slavish reprising of scriptural text), for *ipsissima structura*. The great artist, like the great poet, is one who establishes in and by and through his or her work new criteria for artistic or poetic greatness by establishing a new world in which it *is* such. As one modern writer has expressed it, "a true metaphor is one whose power creates the participation whereby its truth is experienced".

The Prodigal Son's moment of *metanoia* releases in him a discourse and a resolve which is entirely realistic and at the same time is a total denial of all that he has been. As Augustine says of his own painful moment of conversion, "I had known it all along, but I had always pretended that it was something different. I had turned a blind eye and forgotten it." In the event, the boy's father does not even let him utter his prepared speech. In his joy, he cuts words off short in his commands for the celebration, for the highest peaks of self, those moments of most intense consciousness, cannot be analysed or explained in words but only experienced. The son, coming to himself has found himself in the father: that which could not be said has been said, and in the utterance has been wholly absorbed in a new life which has been drawn out of the death which was thought to be life.

The Prodigal must leave himself in order to come back into himself. When our reading of the Bible, and our sense of its authority, threatens to become a self-consuming activity, then it also becomes closed and immobile. Brevard Childs and James Sanders have recognized the need to release the canon from the constraints of a particular historicism and limited perspective. Here we have gone much further, allowing our reading of the Bible to encounter a wide range of literary and artistic activities, so that, leaving itself and its familiar patterns of reception to dally with novelists, artists and film-makers, it may begin to find itself anew. And if some discernible as elder brothers raise their eyebrows, one might remind them that they, in their turn, no doubt, look back to critical prodigals of earlier biblical readings who have returned and become respectable. The common end, one hopes, beyond criticism, is those celebratory acts[15] which recognize the Bible and its intertexts as truly gifts for our salvation, that is our healing as individuals and as groups in a festive encounter with its text.

Notes

1. John Barton, *People of the Book? The Authority of the Bible in Christianity* (London, 1988) pp. 36–8.
2. See ibid., p. 24.
3. Ibid., pp. 19–20, 27.
4. Ibid., p. 59.
5. Robert Alter, *The Art of Biblical Narrative* (London, 1981) ch. 1, pp. 3–22.
6. See Stephen Moore, *Literary Criticism and the Gospels* (New Haven and London, 1989).
7. See also Barton, *People of the Book?*, p. 3.
8. Ibid., pp. 61–2.
9. See ibid., p. 57.

10. Rebecca Adams, in *Religion and Literature,* vol. 25, no. 2 (Summer 1993) 121.
11. The drawing, circa 1645–8, is in the British Museum. The painting, *circa* 1636, is in Dresden, Staatliche Kunstsammhugen Gemäldegalerie.
12. Augustine, *Confessions,* trans. R. S. Pine-Coffin (Harmondsworth, 1961) VIII, 7, p. 169.
13. *Circa* 1668–9, St Petersburg, The Hermitage.
14. *Circa* 1642, Haarlem, Teylers Museum.
15. See also Robert Detweiler, *Breaking the Fall* (London, 1989) pp. 38–40.

10

Conclusion: Art and the Biblical Canon

It is recorded in the apocryphal book II Esdras that God has a conversation with the priest and prophetic scribe Ezra, giving him instructions which Ezra is prompt to obey, for he records as follows:

> I took with me the five men as I had been told, and we went away to the field, and there we stayed. On the next day I heard a voice calling me, which said: "Ezra, open your mouth and drink what I give you." So I opened my mouth, and was handed a cup of what seemed like water, except that its colour was the colour of fire. I took it and drank, and as soon as I had done so my mind began to pour forth a flood of understanding, and wisdom grew greater and greater within me, for I retained my memory unimpaired. I opened my mouth to speak, and I continued to speak unceasingly. The Most High gave understanding to the five men, who took turns at writing down what was said, using characters which they had not known before. They remained at work through the forty days, writing all day, and taking food only at night. But as for me, I spoke all through the day; even at night I was not silent. In the forty days, ninety-four books were written. At the end of the forty days the Most High spoke to me. "Make public the books you wrote first," he said, "to be read by good and bad alike. But the last seventy books are to be kept back, and given to none but the wise among your people. They contain a stream of understanding, a fountain of wisdom, a flood of knowledge." And I did so. (II Esdras 14: 37–48)

What we see here is the establishment of a "double canon",[1] a scripture both public and private. The vast majority of Ezra's divinely inspired books are reserved for the privileged few, who act as interpreters for the majority. In other words, a "canon within the canon" (to use Ernst Kasemann's term) can be seen as the strategic means to power of an educated few, its writtenness granting it an unquestioned authority in the politics of Ezra's post-exilic Israel. One critic, Gerald Bruns, goes so far as to suggest that, in spite of Ezra's claims to divine communication, "the power of the text is not intrinsic to it. On the contrary, the text draws its power from the situation which belongs to a definite history and which is structured by this history to receive just this text as it will no other."[2]

This process of canonization as the result, essentially, of political power struggle gives rise to what is sometimes loosely described as the "catholic" approach to a canonical text which is through the medium of a commentary. Those "outside" the privileged few approach the canon, if at all, only through layers of interpretation. They listen to priestly pronouncements rather than actually read the Bible or, at best, come to the text only under the firm control of methods of reading which actually prevent them from direct exposure to the "incendiary" text itself. The authority of the chosen few, or the "Church" with a capital C, is preserved inviolate. Under Ezra, as powerful priest and ruler as well as prophetic scribe, we receive the notion of canonization as the promotion of a text as sacred and binding – as a matter, therefore, of power.

Thus in the authoritarian state like the Gilead of *The Handmaid's Tale*, the powerless subjects are forbidden to read the Bible, which is kept locked away, available only under the strict supervision of those in authority who read to them. The irony may be, of course, that in such a state, even the powerful are ultimately powerless, the text finally more than the condition granted to it by the politics of its sacralization.

An alternative approach to the text of the canon we may describe as 'protestant', which, un-Ezra-like, tends to play down exclusivity and the problem of *how* to read. Here again, power is a central notion, for protestantism assumes that the canonical book has inherent power to speak to the reader – any reader. Not now the Church, but the Bible itself is the final arbiter, though, as Luther was perfectly well aware, the reading of the Bible is a struggle won only when the Spirit takes hold of the reader in all its power. Luther knew that "the Bible has a wax nose"[3] unless it is read from the citadel of the theological certainty that it is truly the Word of God. In contemporary biblical criticism, the heirs of Luther are the canonical critics, Brevard Childs and James Sanders, whose project, as we have seen, is deeply and disturbingly theological, yet bears witness to precisely the theological necessity of a more literary approach to the Bible. For if the catholic approach tends towards the canon within the canon, the heart of the matter reserved for the wise and good, the protestant approach tends inevitably towards what has been described as the "working canon"[4] within the whole of scripture, that is a selection of texts which are definitive for the interpretation of the whole. Thus, though it would be an error to suppose that Luther was concerned only with the right understanding of a single biblical passage, it is nevertheless true that Luther himself emphasizes that once he had attained a right understanding of Romans 1: 17, the whole Bible took on a new appearance for him. One critic, David Kelsey, gives the game away when he suggests that "although 'canon' is not necessarily a part of the concept 'scripture', 'scripture' is necessarily a part of the meaning of 'canon' " (p. 104). Reading is therefore possible, but it is essentially a selective reading which grants a hermeneutic key to all other reading.

Now, of course, as a cursory review of the history of protestantism quickly indicates, the protestant approach (unlike the catholic approach) is highly vulnerable to the ambiguities of language, especially in translation, and to the demands of different readers at different times and in different circumstances. Sects, each with their own "working canon", abound through the changes and chances of history. For the particular power of the written word in this approach is to establish the self-identity of the community – a process which I have described in an earlier work as "entextualisation", whereby particular uses of scripture are necessary for the shaping and identification of a community. The text forms the community which turns to it for confirmation of its particular orthodoxy. As David Kelsey puts it, "in declaring just these writings 'canon' the church was giving part of a self-description of her identity".[5] Not only may this involve a "working canon" selected from scripture as a whole, but also a range of possible strategies of reading whereby the instabilities of the canonical literature are controlled. Thus, New Testament materials may control readings of the Old Testament, as in Rudolf Bultmann or Brevard Childs: in early Christianity, arguably, the opposite tends to be true, the Old tending to control the New. Karl Barth, on the other hand, tries to maintain the two testaments in a dialectical tension.

All such strategies of reading are attempts to confirm that precious commodity, the "normativity" of the canonical text. In his standard Introduction to the Old Testament, Otto Eissfeldt categorically defines canon (claiming this as the fourth-century Christian sense) as "a book which derives from divine revelation and provides the normative rule for the faith and life of the religious man".[6] True to the tradition of Ezra, Eissfeldt regards the history of the establishment of the canon as beginning with the direct intervention of God and continuing through history. The normativity of the text is maintained under the highest authority, and theology has continued to hold a vested interest in its undisputed role in the religious life. As long as the privileged reader – whether as priest or as critic – is in control of the reading process, the strategic possibilities are almost limitless. And so one recent critic can appear so liberal as to suggest the following:

> Scripture is ... the primary *source* for all subsequent reflection that claims to be Christian. If we accept this, then we are ascribing some sort of normative role to the New Testament. We are not saying that the New Testament is always right; we are not saying that the New Testament is always self-consistent. All that we are saying is that all subsequent Christian reflection and development, if it is to be recognizably Christian, must relate to the New Testament witness in some way way or other. It cannot ignore it.[7]

I perceive all sorts of sleight of hand here. There is the implication of the "canon within the canon" or the "working canon" – read only the bits that the critics tell you are "right". To be a member of the Church you must go back to these books, and, by implication, you need the critic to guide you through them, that is, the modern equivalent of Ezra's "wise among your people". The catholic and the protestant approaches to the set books here join hands in a power game of control over the Bible-reading community. The doctrine of normativity counters the vulnerability of the protestant approach to the uncertainties of language in textuality: these texts are divine in origin and have an inherent power to speak to the reader (under gentle guidance).

Robert Detweiler has suggested that we can summarize the traits of a sacred text under seven headings:

1. claiming or generating claims of divine inspiration;
2. revelatory of divinity;
3. somehow encoded or "hidden";
4. requiring a privileged interpreter;
5. effecting the transformation of lives;

6. the necessary foundation of religious ritual (leading to the confirmation of self-identity);
7. evocative of divine presence.[8]

The net result of this in the process of canonization strikes me as actually not very far removed from the work of contemporary literary critics who, suspicious of traditional ideas of canonicity as an instrument of power, have sought to establish the notion of canon in the reading of "secular" literature. For example, Frank Kermode, writing as an "outsider" to scripture offers an apparently endlessly renewable series of canons in literature responding to the changing pressures of institutional life. His own critical attitude is very much that of a mandarin in his long-term project, since his 1975 T. S. Eliot Memorial Lectures, *The Classic*, of the redemption of the secular classic for modernism: lurking in the background is the sense of the privileged reader who is one of the wise among the people. Or again, much more radically, Edward Said, the steadfast opponent of the notion of canon, proposes instead a new canonical model which has been described as a kind of "canon in transience", a malleable arrangement of texts which adapt to changing cultural demands and circumstances. For all their suspicion of the biblical tradition, with its fixed canon, or their rejection of T. S. Eliot's notion of the privileged "maturity" of the classic texts which constitute his canon of literature (sustained by the great and good through the ages), in his 1944 essay "What is a Classic?", critics like Kermode and Said still, in the words of a recent commentator,

> undertake to create a kind of secular scripture, an imaginative narrative which tells the whole story about the origins, transmission, history, and interrelationships of traditionally valued and customarily neglected works of literary or visual art.[9]

This shift, initiated by a suspicion that a canon is politically exclusive and reserved (a reasonable enough fear following the forty days of Ezra), in fact is merely a move from interest in the canon as *normative* to interest in its function as *narrative*, maintaining all the while the sense of an inherited, enclosed and finally secret story. What remains is the power of texts and their narratives, interpreted for us by professional critics to whom understanding has been given, whether by the Almighty or by the Academy.

But there is a perceptible shift, though I would argue that it has always been there, necessarily, in scripture, through the energy which, more than the power politics of shamans, priests, prophets or popes, has sustained the biblical tradition in religion, culture and society. We can discern it in that extraordinary and much-quoted conclusion of Kermode's *The Genesis of Secrecy*, which looks back so sadly to Kafka's great parable of the doorkeeper:

> World and book, it may be, are hopelessly plural, endlessly disappointing; we stand alone before them, aware of their arbitrariness and impenetrability, knowing that they may be narratives only because of our impudent intervention, and susceptible of interpretation only by our hermetic tricks. Hot for secrets, our only conversation may be with guardians who know less and see less than we can; and our sole hope and pleasure is in the perception of a momentary radiance,before the door of disappointment is finally shut on us.[10]

The priest-professor sadly admits his limitations and longings, his failure of knowledge, and it is a terrible confession. But what here is demanded is a recognition that the terms of our conversation must be renovated in a shift from text to reader: not a dependence on the political power of the text, but a recognition of the politics of reading in a new and lively interaction and conversation between text and reader who abandons the futile task of waiting before the door of final interpretation which is never opened. It never has been, its truth, the "truth" of canonical authority, merely the expression of a moment when a text becomes sacred when a section of the community is able to establish it as such in order to gain control over the whole community. Instead we must shift our concerns from dependence on the sacred text to the activity of religious reading, ushering in a different kind of politics which is reactive to situations of power and establishment, truly concerned with issues of freedom, the liberation of values, and the endless, democratic exercise of reading as celebratory.

What I am proposing is a "canon" which sustains an endless plurality of readings that reject the notion of insiders and outsiders which has sustained canonicity since Ezra's ninety-four books (of which seventy rest on the reserved shelves), or Mark 4, which emphasizes the difference between the privileged insiders and those outside to whom everything comes in parables ("lest they might turn to God and be forgiven"; v. 12), or Kermode's *The Genesis of Secrecy*. Instead, I recognize that all communication occurs only *within* a context – that all is context, and there is nothing outside the text (which is not, as Kevin Hart has pointed out, a Derridean formalism[11]), and that all understanding between text and reader or between reader and reader is specific only to the occasion and determinate only within its confines. And *that*, as Stanley Fish has recognized, is fine, since he complains that his critical opponents in pursuit of their privileged knowledge do not realize

> that such an understanding is enough and that the more perfect understanding they desire – an understanding that operates above or across situations – would have no place in the world even if it were available, because it is only in situations – with their interested specifications as to what counts as a fact, what it is possible to say, what will be heard as an argument – that one is called on to understand.[12]

As we move from sacred text to the notion of religious reading of the canon, we do not, I suggest, shift into mere relativism, but from the authority of the text to the authority of the interpretative community where communication does occur with confidence which has its source in beliefs which are truly communal and conventional.

Now this may seem rather like a new Reformation, but the difference from the "protestant" notion of canon is that it does not depend, unlike Luther, upon the privileging of text or particular texts as the final divine arbiter of religion. On the contrary, its model, idealistic and infinitely fragile and shifting, is closer to Bakhtin's carnivalesque reading of Rabelais. A characteristic of Rabelais' style, Bakhtin remarks, is its tendency to disintegrate quickly in the hands of imitators, losing its universalism and "fullness of life". Once it tends towards the abstract it loses its vigour and its abundance. I deliberately choose Bakhtin's *Rabelais and His World* (1965) because he uses it as a weapon against the deathly tendencies of institutionalization, whether in the Church or in the State. For in the end the Bible also remains to be encountered as an antidote to the consequences of the processes of its own canonization in the tradition. Bakhtin reacts strongly against all notions of inside/outside, against the elimination of laughter from the religious cult in a condemnation which goes back to Tertullian, Cyprian and John Chrysostom.[13] The liturgy and official worship of the Church effectively excluded all rudiments of gaiety and laughter in their authorizations of practice. For laughter is subversive, and excessive, opposed ultimately to "the monolith of the Christian cult and ideology".

Just as the biblical texts moved from story to sacred text, so the Christian Church adapted feasts, taming them for its own purposes. My sense is that within these "sacred" occasions remains an energy which is the true heart of scripture – that is, writings available for endless exchanges within acts of religious reading which continue through the tradition in spite of the periodic and continually re-formed strategies which move to "sacralize" the texts in the interests of party, prince or priest. Robert Detweiler, to whom much of what I am saying is deeply indebted, suggests two German terms which may be central to the interpretative communities which celebrate such celebratory readings. The first was used in the fourteenth century by Meister Eckhart, and has been picked up in our own time by Heidegger. It is *Gelassenheit* – loosely translated as "calmness" or "abandonment", a serenity in the face of whatever life offers. The second is *geselligkeit* – roughly, "sociability" or "communality". Detweiler sums these words up with the suggestion that

> Religious reading might be *gelassen* and *gesellig*, balancing our dogged insistence on interpretation with a pleasurable interchange made valuable precisely by a refusal to simplify and manipulate the text into something else, another statement.[14]

I should make it plain that when I talk of "religious reading" I am not simply meaning reading in the narrow sense of literacy. That would, of course, exclude the vast majority of those through the ages who could not read written words in this sense. Religious reading is that interaction with scripture which includes responses to visual art, music or drama. It maintains the vitality of the text, its narratives and stories, its lyrics and its tragedy through re-presentation and re-interpretation in conversation, worship and performance. It sustains its universality, and therefore its history, in a radical comedy of an affirmative community which may be parodic, grotesque, tragic, but is always regenerative of these texts which form the Bible.

I would argue also that a "canon" consists precisely of those texts which continue to provoke and sustain religious readings. This will, from day to day, always involve "canons within canons" or "working canons", but the survival of the Bible as a whole (always a somewhat unstable notion, though always at the same time tending towards stability), depends upon a unity which exists precisely because it entertains its own deconstruction in reading and performance, a scandalous quality derived from its own excess as (in D. H. Lawrence's words) "a great confused novel", or in Milan Kundera a living "art born of the laughter of God".[15]

What, then, are the characteristics of reading religiously? Deeply playful, it is conducted in an atmosphere of celebration – of Bakhtin's carnival. There is nothing more serious than this, as a response to and encounter with text. It lies at the very heart of all liturgical celebration, though its power is too often usurped for institutional stability in the interests of normativity. But it is why, in the Middle Ages, the English drama, which began at the Easter Sepulchres in church sanctuaries slipped away from the sacred building into the market place where more vigorously the universal, synchronic text could playfully and tragically encounter the particular and the diachronic in the festive performance of the Miracle Cycles.

In such contexts reading ceases to be either a singular encounter of the lonely reader with the sacred text, or the imposition of a reading upon a passive congregation, but a group celebration in which all have their part to play in a genuine anamnesis or re-creation. Even in such a humble activity as my young daughters' nursery school nativity play, I recognize that, for them (and therefore for the devoted parents watching) they really *are* angels and shepherds, in all their clumsiness, embarrassment and excitement reliving the sense of the gospel narratives. And it gets harder and harder for us to re-enact this as we grow more demanding theologically and more cynical in community. So the text slips away from us, and we demand those who can interpret it for us.

Religious reading is thus one which celebrates the text. That is, it interacts with and *enacts* the text, both affirming its enduring importance and playfully deconstructing tendencies hermeneutically to reduce its excess and its ambiguity. We can describe this as a creative way of realizing the surplus of meaning in such a text, and its unwillingness to be defined by conclusion or dogma. The text is always more than anything we can say about it, and that is precisely its value, since it frustrates our claims to knowledge and invites us into a vision of which we are a part as we "read". In this sense, a text's "textuality" might be described as its "personality" – that which renders a person with whom we exchange conversation beyond mere definition, infinitely mysterious and always worthwhile.

Such a surplus of meaning is dealt with in the business of metaphor, whose energy is never spent and which leads us ever into new adventures of understanding and imagination. Metaphor bears witness to the excess of life in texts, and nowhere is the life of metaphor more abundant than in the Bible, which, I would suggest, is one good reason why it has endured both constructively as a canon and deconstructively as a classic in the literary history of the West. Metaphors, as Paul Ricoeur reminds us in *La métaphore vive* (1975) are endlessly creative of meaning, metaphor calling to metaphor in limitless succession giving energy to that which theology and dogma tend to ossify. In religious reading, it may be said, we find our true being as Ricoeur concludes that

> the "place" of metaphor, its most intimate and ultimate abode, is neither the name, nor the sentence, nor even discourse, but the copula of the verb *to be*. The metaphorical "is" at once signifies both "is not" and "is like". If this is really so, we are allowed to speak of metaphorical truth, but in an equally "tensive" sense of the word "truth".[16]

Finally, religious reading explores what Detweiler describes both as an "intensity of form" and the "*irreduceability* of form". That is, it takes, in its playfulness, the text absolutely seriously, without concern to coerce it for political gain, or read through it for the establishment of system. For it recognizes that this is all there is, this, if you like is IT, in the joyful celebration of an interaction which is universal yet affirms the individual, which laughs for sheer joy and confirms the interpretative community as a genuine community of the many in the one, never concluded and never exclusive. At the same time, it allows common utterance of that experience which is, in other terms, incommunicable and beyond words of definition, the experience of pain which isolates and finally kills.

Why these texts? My answer to that is because these texts, the books of the biblical canon, have the capacity like no other collection of texts in the Western tradition, to embrace a multitude of texts which celebrate their canonicity. The Bible should not be read exclusively and outside the tradition of art and literature into which it expands and which it absorbs. This is, it seems to me, far more significant than all the methodologies of reading and systems and theologies which have claimed the Bible as their ultimate authority. It breaks the encoded secrecy of Ezra's seventy books. As Northrop Frye once expressed it (though I am deeply suspicious of his own canonizing procedures):

> The Bible is the supreme example of the way that myths can, under certain social pressures stick together to make up a mythology. A second look at this mythology shows us that it actually became, for medieval and later centuries, a vast mythological universe, stretching in time from creation to apocalypse, and in metaphorical space from heaven to hell. A mythological universe is a vision of reality in terms of human concerns and hopes and anxieties: it is not a primitive form of science.[17]

Scripture gives rise to a secular scripture which both deconstructs and validates by deconstructing its canonicity. Let me conclude by illustrating what I mean in a particular example from the Gospel of Luke 2: 8–17, which comes to my mind since as I write it is now only two days to Christmas. It is one of the most familiar and best-loved passages in the New Testament. I use the Authorized Version:

> And there were in the same country shepherds abiding in the fields, keeping watch over their flock by night. And, lo, the angel of the Lord came upon them, and the glory of the Lord shone round about them: and they were sore afraid. And the angel said unto them, Fear not: for, behold, I bring you good tidings of great joy, which shall be to all people. For unto you is born this day in the city of David a Saviour, which is Christ the Lord. And this shall be a sign unto you: Ye shall find the babe wrapped in swaddling clothes, lying in a manger. And suddenly there was with the angel a multitude of the heavenly host praising God, and saying, Glory to God in the highest, and on earth peace, good will toward men. And it came to pass, as the angels were gone away from them into heaven, the shepherds said to one another, Let us now go even unto Bethlehem, and see this thing which is come to pass, which the Lord hath made known to us. And they came with haste, and found Mary, and Joseph, and the babe lying in a manger. And when they had seen it, they made known abroad the saying which was told them concerning this child.

In the early fifteenth century in Wakefield, England, the so-called *Secunda Pastorum,* or *Second Shepherds' Play* of the Towneley Cycle of miracle plays, takes this passage out of the sanctuary of the church and places it on the pageant wagon of the tradesmen of the town. Most of the play is a delicious parody of the nativity scene in the story of Mak the sheep-stealer and his wife Gill, who tries to hide a lamb by placing it in a crib. The play concludes with the visit of the shepherds to the real manger in a tone of suitable devotion. Here brilliant "secular" drama becomes an intertext with the Gospel which places our reading of it at the heart of a comic vision that intensifies and "realizes" the biblical passage with a humane intensity that liturgy tends to attenuate. The worship of the shepherds at the manger leads us, readers or audience, in a worship which is a celebration of the text, and a situating of its spirit within the comedy of our appreciation and laughter. As Detweiler describes this experience, it "provides an avenue toward uncovering a sacredness of language always present in our liturgies, but largely suppressed in the reference-orientation of our worship".[18]

But we do not have to refer to the fifteenth century for the continuing energy of this moment of the gospel narrative. Here is a modern American poem by Peter Meinke, "The Gift of the Magi":

> The angel of the Lord sang low
> and shucked his golden slipper off
> and stretched his wings as if to show
> their starlit shadow on the wall
> and did the old soft shoe, yea,
> did the buck and wing.
>
> The Magi put their arms around
> each other, then with chorus line
> precision and enormous zest
> they kicked for Jesus onetwothree
> high as any Christmas tree
> and Caspar was the best.
>
> And Melchior told a story that
> had Joseph sighing in the hay
> while Holy Mary rolled her eyes
> and Jesus smiling where he lay
> as if he understood, Lord,
> knew the joke was good.

But Balthazar began to weep
foreseeing all the scenes to come:
the Child upon a darker stage
the star, their spotlight, stuttering out –
then shook his head, smiled, and sang
louder than before.

There was no dignity that night:
the shepherds slapped their sheepish knees
and tasted too much of the grape
that solaces our sober earth
O blessèd be our mirth, hey!
Blessèd be our mirth![19]

Meinke continues to celebrate in the idiom of the twentieth century, more freely than the medieval playwright dare bringing his comedy into the Holy Family itself. Yet his poem maintains the unity through the ages of celebration, each poet joined to the other in being true to himself, and all sustaining the wonder of the Gospel verses, a wonder too often at risk in the fastidiousness of theology with its desire to protect the Holy Family from the humour and even the tipsiness of the everyday. The poets sustain and celebrate that "modern oblivion" of sacred obsession. Art has never shunned this vigorous defence of biblical life which even such a one as Charles Dickens, in his defence of the "purity" of religion in the Victorian age, described as "odious, repulsive, and revolting" as against "associations" which are "tender, awful, sorrowful, ennobling, sacred, graceful, or beautiful".[20]

But who, in the end, is the custodian of such things? Is it really the custodian of the sacred text who is more concerned to establish an authority of orthodoxy, a division between those within and those outside? Surely religious reading and theology in the end is more than that! So let me turn, as I so often do, to the painter Rembrandt for a final word on Luke 2: 9–17. In the history of art, the shepherds are not central characters until the sixteenth century, until then being generally only observers in the background as the child is worshipped by Mary. But in the humanism of Rembrandt the profound human mystery and warmth of the Gospel are fully discovered. In the great canvas painted about 1646, and commissioned by Frederik Henrik, the Prince of Orange, Rembrandt eliminates all angels or heavenly figures. It is an entirely domestic scene in which the shepherds kneel or stand, some huddling their arms for warmth, gazing upon a tiny baby in the light of a stable lantern and a candle which Joseph holds for their benefit. I am struck in particular by Mary, who is a real, capable mother, quite unlike the typical dreamy madonna of art. The realism of this picture in no way detracts from the profound dignity of the scene, which is the dignity of a scarred, peasant humanity.

But, as so frequently with Rembrandt, I am even more moved by a later rough etching dating from about 1654, in which there are no concessions to the roughness of the stable, even to the somehow comic image of Joseph having only an upturned wheelbarrow to sit on. Here, the shepherds are eagerly crowding over the wooden division of the stable, one carrying his bagpipes, another holding back a small child who is a little too eager to see. In its utter simplicity and human warmth, this takes us straight back to a reading of Luke 2, filling in its indeterminacies without aggression and without imposition. Thus, in this tradition, the text of the Gospel becomes sacred not through the exercise of power, but through a textual empathy between the evangelist, the medieval playwright, Peter Meinke and Rembrandt. Of course interpretation is taking place, which will tend to create a sacred text, but it remains legitimate only because its interpretative claims are born out by the text which continues to inspire and be inspired.

Any sacred text, any canon, will establish a hermeneutic circle of interpretation and sacrality – interpretation creating authoritative (sacred) texts, and authoritative (sacred) texts compelling interpretation. But, as Heidegger recognized, if a hermeneutic circle is inevitable, what is important is not how you get out of it (which I doubt you can do), but how you enter the circle. Shall we enter with violence, and with the desire to establish that *our* reading is correct, or with the imperative that all others either read as we do, or even simply meekly follow without reading, guided by the superior wisdom of others? Or shall we enter with the poets and artists (and one should add the musicians, remembering the deep influence of such works as Handel's *Messiah* upon the popular culture of my own northern England), with humour and a sense of the ordinariness of the eternal and the humanity of the divine subject? Over the years since my days as a student of theology, I have become more and more convinced that one was taught to begin at the wrong end, with dire consequences of one sort or another.

If in our worship and religious reading of scripture we become increasingly uneasy with the notion of reference in a celebration where sacred presence is increasingly felt as an illusion, does this simply then spell the end of the sacred text? Has the canon of our reading religiously moved us beyond that "sense" which apparently gave rise to the writings of the Bible, the presence of divinity? Even as I finish, I am not sure that I have any clear response to that, in spite of all I have said. I am sure that the notion of reading religiously is something we never actually fully realize, for we will always tend to fall back into our old ways – any canon always assuming some "presence" whether that be divine or academic or political in a narrow sense. But precisely this sense of presence which a canonical literature will at least suggest, should also inspire a suspicion which takes us not away from the text in the establishment of the authoritative "truth" of presence, but back more vigorously to the act of reading which deconstructs that presence and restores, between its immanence and transcendence, a *Geselligkeit,* a sociability, and *Gelassenheit,* serenity of freedom. Thus the canon both binds and frees, freeing us from its binding and binding us to freedom in the joyful act of reading. That is exactly what is happening in Rembrandt's pictures of the adoration of the shepherds. So in Meinke's poem we are free to laugh because we know this is utterly serious.

A few moments ago I referred to Ricoeur's sense of the metaphorical as abiding tensively in the copula of the verb *to be*. I wonder, in conclusion, if this sense of "being" is entirely adequate to what I have been suggesting. For the shift from an emphasis on text to the notion of religious reading takes us also from an emphasis on being to something much more deliberately suspended between text and reader, across the space made by reading in which is stressed "the importance of this nothingness which is neither being (a something) nor non-being (nihilism), but which is the play-between".[21] In such play, seriously engaged in with texts that endlessly tolerate the claims of reading religiously, we begin to sense the true end of reading which is a reading of the unreadable, not in Kermode's sense of an unfollowable world, but in a reading which moves joyously beyond the claims of the written word in *communitas* and love. In prosaic terms, this is to realize that the canonical criticism of Brevard Childs and James Sanders is witness to the theological necessity of a more literary approach to the Bible. More specifically, it is an acknowledgement that only in texts, and perhaps only *these* texts, are continually evoked those celebratory acts in communion which take us out of ourselves, and out of all our strategies of power and domination, in order to come to the other in humility, friendship, humour and love.

Notes

1. See Gerald L. Bruns, "Canon and Power in Hebrew Scriptures", *Critical Inquiry*, vol. 10, no. 3 (1984) 462–80.
2. Ibid., 466. See also Robert Detweiler, "What Is a Sacred Text?", *Semeia*, vol. 31 (1985) 213–30.
3. See Gerhard Ebeling, *Luther: An Introduction to His Thought*, trans. R. A. Wilson (London, 1972) p. 97.
4. See David H. Kelsey, *The Uses of Scripture in Recent Theology* (London, 1975) p. 104.
5. Ibid., p. 105.
6. Otto Eissfeldt, *The Old Testament: An Introduction*, trans. Peter R. Ackroyd (Oxford, 1966) p. 560.
7. Christopher Tuckett, *Reading the New Testament: Methods of Interpretation* (London, 1987) p. 18.
8. Detweiler, "What Is a Sacred Text?", p. 223.
9. Jan Gorak, *The Making of the Modern Canon: Genesis and Crisis of a Literary Idea* (London and Atlantic Highlands, 1991) p. 260.
10. Frank Kermode, *The Genesis of Secrecy: On the Interpretation of Narrative* (Cambridge, Mass., and London, 1979) p. 145.
11. Kevin Hart, *The Trespass of the Sign* (Cambridge, 1989) pp. 25–6.
12. Stanley Fish, *Is There a Text in This Class? The Authority of Interpretive Communities* (Cambridge, Mass., and London, 1980) p. 304.
13. See Mikhail Bakhtin, *Rabelais and His World*, trans. Helene Iswolsky (Bloomington, 1984) ch. 1: "Rabelais in the History of Laughter".
14. Robert Detweiler, *Breaking the Fall* (London, 1981) p. 35.
15. See Milan Kundera, *The Art of the Novel* (London, 1990).
16. Paul Ricoeur, *The Rule of Metaphor* (Toronto, 1977) p. 7.
17. Northrop Frye, *The Secular Scripture* (Cambridge, Mass., and London, 1978) p. 14.
18. Detweiler, *Breaking the Fall*, p. 58.
19. Peter Meinke, *Liquid Paper* (Pittsburgh and London, 1991) p. 112.
20. Charles Dickens, quoted in Humphry House, *The Dickens World*, 2nd edn (1942; Oxford, 1960) p. 126. See also p. 64.
21. See David Miller, "Play Not", in Mark Ledbetter and David Jasper (eds), *In Good Company: Essays in Honor of Robert Detweiler* (Atlanta, 1994).

Bibliography

The following brief bibliography is in no sense exhaustive. It offers a guide to some of the more important studies in "canonical criticism", and the books which have shaped each chapter.

CANONICAL CRITICISM

Childs, Brevard S., *Old Testament Theology in a Canonical Context* (London, 1985).

——, *The New Testament as Canon: An Introduction* (Philadelphia, 1985).

Sanders, James A., *Canon and Community: A Guide to Canonical Criticism* (Philadelphia, 1984).

——, *From Sacred Story to Sacred Text: Canon as Paradigm* (Philadelphia, 1987).

Wall, Robert W. and Eugene E. Lemcio (eds), *The New Testament as Canon: A Reader in Canonical Criticism. Journal for the Study of the New Testament*, Supplement Series 76 (Sheffield, 1992).

GENERAL

Altizer, Thomas J. J., *Genesis and Apocalypse* (Louisville, 1990) [Chapter 8].

Babington Bruce and Peter William Evans, *Biblical Epics: Sacred Narrative in the Hollywood Cinema* (Manchester, 1993) [Chapter 6].

Bal, Mieke, *Reading "Rembrandt": Beyond the World–Image Opposition* (Cambridge, 1991) [Chapter 4].

Barton, John, *People of the Book? The Authority of the Bible in Christianity* (London, 1988) [Chapter 9].

Baudrillard, Jean, *The Evil Demon of Images*, trans. Paul Patton and Paul Foss (Sydney, 1987) [Chapter 7].

Budick, Sanford and Wolfgang Iser (eds), *Languages of the Unsayable: The Play of Negativity in Literature and Literary Theory* (New York, 1989) [Chapter 6].

Detweiler, Robert, *Breaking the Fall* (London, 1991) [Chapter 10].

——, "What is a Sacred Text?", *Semeia*, vol. 31 (1985) 213–30 [Chapter 10].

Gorak, Jan, *The Making of the Modern Canon: Genesis and Crisis of a Literary Idea* (London, 1991).

Hoekstra, Hidde, *Rembrandt and the Bible* (Utrecht, 1990) [Chapter 4].

Kermode, Frank, *Poetry, Narrative History* (Oxford, 1990).

Kermode, Frank and Robert Alter (eds), *The Literary Guide to the Bible* (London, 1987).
Kroker, Arthur and David Cook, *The Postmodern Scene* (London, 1988) [Chapter 7].
le Doeuff, Michèle, *Hipparchia's Choice: An Essay Concerning Women, Philosophy, Etc.*, trans. Trista Selous (Oxford, 1991) [Chapter 5].
McLuhan, Marshall, *Understanding Media: The Extensions of Man* (London and New York, 1964) [Chapter 6].
Steinberg, Leo, *The Sexuality of Christ in Renaissance Art and in Modern Oblivion* (New York, 1983) [Chapter 4].
Tracy, David, *The Analogical Imagination: Christian Theology and the Culture of Pluralism* (London, 1981).
Weinsheimer, Joel, *Philosophical Hermeneutics and Literary Theory* (New Haven and London, 1991).

Index

www.ingramcontent.com/pod-product-compliance
Lightning Source LLC
LaVergne TN
LVHW050645100826
845148LV00011B/1983

* 9 7 8 1 6 0 6 0 8 8 3 5 7 *